The Most Crucial Knots to Know

Step-by-Step Guide How to Tie 40+ Knots
for Camping, Survival, and Preppers

Aaron Linsdau

Sastrugi Press
Jackson, WY

©2021 Aaron Linsdau
Interior image copyrights © Aaron Linsdau
Cover images © Aaron Linsdau

The Most Crucial Knots to Know: Step-by-Step Guide How to Tie 40+ Knots for Camping, Survival, and Preppers

All rights reserved. No part of this book may be reproduced or transmitted in any form or by any means, electronic or mechanical, including photocopying, recording, or by any information storage and retrieval system without the written permission of the author, except where permitted by law.

Sastrugi Press / Published by arrangement with the author
Sastrugi Press: PO Box 1297, Jackson, WY 83001, United States www.sastrugipress.com

The activities described in this book are inherently dangerous. The publisher does not have any control over and does not assume any responsibility for author or third-party websites or their content.

Modern medical treatment is a constantly evolving field—recommended treatment and drug therapy are always changing. All medical treatment discussed in this book must be evaluated using the most current product information provided by the manufacturer to verify the recommended dose, the proper administration, and contraindications. It is always the responsibility of the licensed practitioner, relying on training and knowledge of the patient, to determine the best treatment and proper dosages for each individual. Neither the publisher nor the author assume any liability for any injury or illness related to the medical discussions in this publication.

Any person participating in the activities described in this work is personally responsible for learning the proper techniques and using good judgment. You are responsible for your own actions and decisions. The information contained in this work is subjective and based solely on opinions. No book can advise you of all potential hazards or anticipate the limitations of any reader. Participation in the described activities can result in severe injury or death. Neither the publisher nor the author assume any liability for anyone participating in the activities described in this work.

Trademarks are property of their respective owners. The mention of any product in this book is not an endorsement of the product. The manufacturer of any product mentioned in this book is not an endorsement of this book.

Library of Congress Cataloging-in-Publication Data

Names: Linsdau, Aaron, author.
Title: The most crucial knots to know : step-by-step guide how to tie 40+
  knots for camping, survival, and preppers / Aaron Linsdau.
Description: Jackson, WY : Sastrugi Press, [2021]
Identifiers: LCCN 2021058817 (print) | LCCN 2021058818 (ebook) | ISBN
  9781649222268 (paperback) | 9781649222251 (hardback)
Subjects: LCSH: Knots and splices. | Wilderness survival--Equipment and
  supplies. | Camping--Equipment and supplies.
Classification: LCC TT840.R66 L56 2021 (print) | LCC TT840.R66 (ebook) |
  DDC 746.42/2--dc23/eng/20211220
LC record available at https://lccn.loc.gov/2021058817
LC ebook record available at https://lccn.loc.gov/2021058818

15 14 13 12 11 10 9 8

Contents

Introduction 5
Terminology 6
Suggested Learning Order 7
Knots 8
    Albright Knot 8
    Alpine Butterfly Knot 10
    Bowline Knot 12
    Bowline on a Bight 14
    Cat's Paw 16
    Cleat Hitch 18
    Clove Hitch 20
    Constrictor Knot 22
    Double Fisherman's Bend 24
    Double Overhand Stopper Knot 28
    Figure 8 Knot 30
    Figure 8 Bend (Flemish Bend) 32
    Figure 8 Follow Through Loop 36
    Figure 8 on a Bight 40
    Flat Overhand Bend 42
    Girth Hitch 44
    Highwayman's Hitch 46
    Honda Knot (Lariat) 48
    Improved Clinch Knot 50
    Lark's Head (Cow Hitch) 52
    Marlinspike Hitch 54
    Miller's Knot 56
    Mooring Hitch 58
    Munter Hitch 60
    Overhand Bight 62
    Overhand Knot (Half Hitch) 64
    Palomar Knot 66
    Pipe Hitch 68
    Prusik Knot 70
    San Diego Jam Knot 72
    Sheet Bend 74

    SHOELACE BOW 76
    SIBERIAN HITCH (PACKER'S KNOT) 78
    SLIP KNOT 80
    SQUARE KNOT 82
    STEVEDORE STOPPER KNOT 84
    TAUT-LINE HITCH 86
    TIMBER HITCH 88
    TRUCKER'S HITCH 90
    TUMBLE HITCH 92
    TWO HALF-HITCHES 94
    WATER KNOT 96

Lashings 98
    DIAGONAL LASHING 98
    ROUND LASHING 100
    SHEAR LASHING 102
    SQUARE LASHING 104
    TRIPOD LASHING 106
    BACK SPLICE 108
    EYE SPLICE 110
    WHIPPING 112

Rigs & Climbing 114
    SLED TOWING RIG 114
    SWISS SEAT 116
    TEXAS PRUSIK 120
    ROPE CARE & TYPES 122

Scenarios 124
    KNOT TYING SCENARIOS 124
    SURVIVAL TIPS 127

About the Author 128
Other Books by the Author 129

Introduction

Learning to tie knots and applying them to daily life is a rewarding experience. They can be used to render first aid to save a life or simply to hold a clothesline to dry laundry. Knots have as many varied uses as there are stars visible in the sky.

Choosing the correct knot for the job is often the greatest challenge. Which one to choose? What knots can save a life? Can one get away with a simple overhand knot for everything?

Countless books and online resources share a bewildering forest of knots. This book targets those who want the most useful knots for daily living, outdoor pursuits, survival, and preparing for the unknown. Each knot is professionally photographed and annotated. The question this book answers is: Which knot to choose and when?

Understanding how to tie a knot is a matter of memorization and practice. Learning the wisdom of when and where to apply the knot is the crucial skill this book teaches the reader.

Most knots were developed with a specific use in mind. Each knot description notes their ideal application. Some are easier to tie or untie than others. In an emergency, having a few knots available in memory can make all the difference in survival.

All knots reduce a rope's strength. There is no way around this. Whatever the application of the knot, ensure that the rope is more than sufficient for the job. This is especially important for climbing and overhead lifting. A little more strength never hurt.

Over the centuries, knot names have changed, causing confusion. This book uses the most common names and tying styles to help eliminate that tangle of language. The text follows classic conventions to make learning easy and quick.

Survivalists, preppers, and outdoor enthusiasts will cherish this book as a valuable resource. It is a solid text for adults and children alike. Knowing how to create a tool out of simple rope will make all the difference in life's unexpected moments.

—Aaron Linsdau

 THE MOST CRUCIAL KNOTS TO KNOW

Terminology

BIGHT: A bight is a U-shaped tight curve

DRESSING A KNOT: Tightening and finishing a knot or hitch so it is snug with no loose strands or loops.

HITCHES VS KNOTS: Knots are usually tied between two ropes or to themselves. Hitches are usually tied to an object.

LASHING: A method of tying two objects, usually poles, together.

LOOP: A loop is when the running end is laid over or placed under the standing part of the rope.

ROUNDTURN: A full turn around an object that brings the running end to the standing part.

RUNNING END: The running end is the part of the rope that is used to tie the knot.

STANDING PART: The standing part of the rope is the opposite of the running end. This part of the rope carries the load.

TAG END: Short end of the line, usually on a fishing knot, that is to be cut off when the knot is dressed.

TAIL: The tail of a rope is the very end of the rope after the knot or hitch is tied.

WRAP OR TURN: A wrap is a 360° turn in the rope around an object.

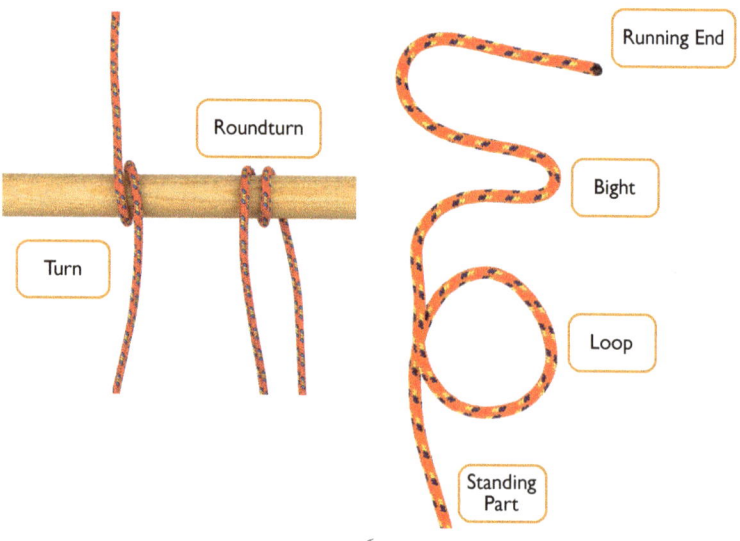

Suggested Learning Order

Which are the most valuable and useful knots to learn first? What knots can the reader get by with while forgoing the others? The below list is broken into three groups as a suggestion on which to learn first. In each grouping, the knots are listed alphabetically.

Learn First

Bowline Knot
Clove Hitch
Figure 8 Knot
Lark's Head (Cow Hitch)
Overhand Bight
Overhand Knot (Half Hitch)
Palomar Knot
Sheet Bend
Shoelace Bow
Slip Knot
Square Knot
Taut-Line Hitch
Timber Hitch
Two Half-Hitches

Learn Second

Alpine Butterfly Knot
Bowline on a Bight
Cat's Paw
Cleat Hitch
Constrictor Knot
Double Fisherman's Bend
Double Overhand Stopper Knot
Figure 8 Bend (Flemish Bend)
Figure 8 Follow Through Loop
Figure 8 on a Bight
Girth Hitch
Improved Clinch Knot
Prusik Knot
Water Knot
Miller's Knot
Mooring Hitch
Munter Hitch

Learn Third

Albright Knot
Back Splice
Diagonal Lashing
Eye Splice
Flat Overhand Bend
Highwayman's Hitch
Honda Knot (Lariat)
Marlinspike Hitch
Pipe Hitch
Round Lashing
San Diego Jam Knot
Shear Lashing
Siberian Hitch (Packer's Knot)
Sled Towing Rig
Square Lashing
Stevedore Stopper Knot
Swiss Seat
Texas Prusik
Tripod Lashing
Trucker's Hitch
Tumble Hitch
Whipping

 THE MOST CRUCIAL KNOTS TO KNOW

Albright Knot

- Tie together two fishing lines
- Works well with slippery lines
- Tie two lines together of different thickness

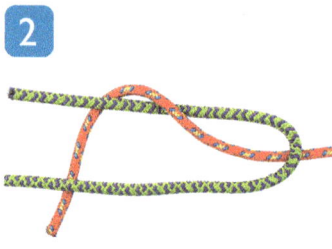

1) Create a bight with the heavier fishing line and place the thinner line (often the leader) under the bight.

2) Begin wrapping the thin line around the neck of the bight of the thick line.

10X

3) Continue wrapping the thin line around the thick line for a total of at least 10 wraps.

4) Thread the running end of the thin line through the bight of the thick line.

5) Moisten the knot. Hold onto both ends and pull on the knot to tighten it. Make sure the loops do not overlap.

6) Dress the knot by pushing the loops together while pulling on the two lines. Cut the tag ends of both lines.

Where & When to Use

The Albright Knot is the perfect choice when you need to tie a leader to a main fishing line. If the main line is braided and the leader is of monofilament or fluorocarbon, this knot is the perfect one to use. Create the loop in the main line and then create the wraps with the thinner, more slippery monofilament or fluorocarbon fishing lines.

Should you be using a line that is exceedingly slippery, this knot will work as a final resort compared to other knots like the Sheet Bend, Double Fisherman's, Figure 8 Bend, etc. This knot takes more time and effort to tie. Once tightened, it is difficult to pull apart. It is intended to be semi-permanent. To remove the leader, cut the knot to separate the lines.

 THE MOST CRUCIAL KNOTS TO KNOW

Alpine Butterfly Knot

- Create a strong loop in the middle of a rope
- Relatively easy to untie after loading
- Excellent climbing and safety knot
- Isolate a damaged section of rope
- Shorten a rope

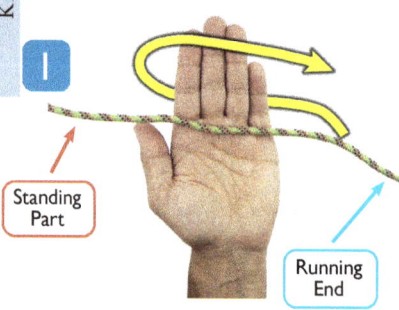

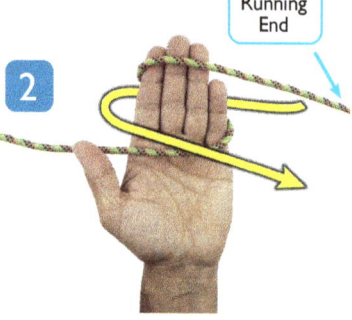

1) Lay the rope across your hand with the running end on the right. Wrap the running end behind and upward around your hand once.

2) Wrap the running end behind and downward around your hand a second time.

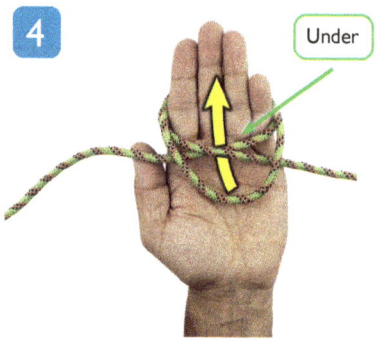

3) Pull the top loop downward and over the two crossed lines of the standing part and running end.

4) Take the loop you pulled down and thread it upward under the two crossed lines of the standing part and running end.

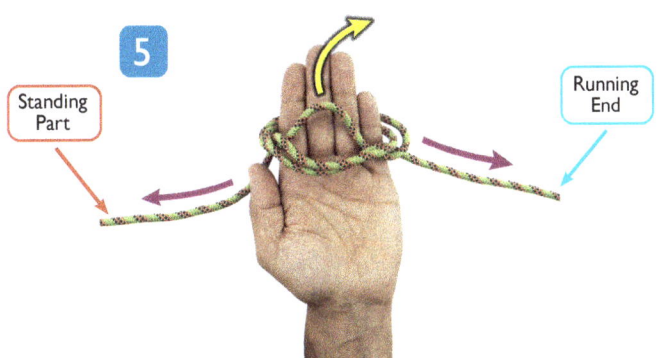

5) Lift the center loop upward with your right hand to tighten the knot. Pull your left hand out of the loops while holding the top loop in your right hand. Begin snugging the standing part and running end.

6) Dress the knot by pushing the loops over the standing part and running ends together while pulling upward on the main loop.

Where & When to Use

The Alpine Butterfly Knot is one of the best and safest knots to create a loop in the middle of a rope. It is used by climbers to clip into the middle of a line while climbing or traveling across glaciers. This is a knot that climbers, spelunkers, and adventurers use to protect their lives.

This knot is also an excellent choice for isolating a damaged piece of rope. It is far stronger and safer than either the Sheepshank or Trumpet Knot for rope shortening.

The knot balances quite well. It can manage an axial load along the standing part to the running end as well as a side load from the loop itself. This knot is a good optional choice to create a loop for the Trucker's Hitch.

The Most Crucial Knots to Know

Bowline Knot

- Scouting knot
- Easy to untie after it is loaded
- Create a loop at the end of a rope
- Doesn't slip under moderate loads

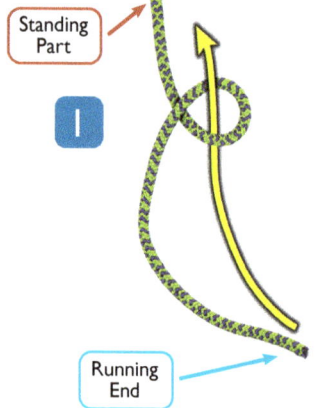

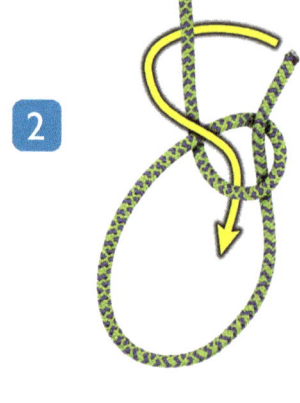

1) Start with a loop over the standing part. Pass the running end through the back of the loop.

2) Pass the running end behind and around the standing part. Continue pulling the running end through the original small loop.

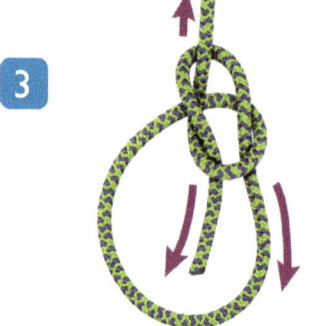

3) Pull upward on the standing part and downward on the running end and right side of the main loop to dress the knot.

4) Dress and snug the knot.

5) Add an Overhand Knot to the running end around the loop for added security.

Security

Where & When to Use

The Bowline Knot is one of the Scouting knots. Use this knot when you want to create a loop at the end of a rope that's easy to untie. It is useful for securing tarps, certain sail rigging, clotheslines, and other times when you need a knot that doesn't slip. It is difficult to tie or untie with a load on the standing part.

The Bowline is a great general-purpose camping knot to secure items with a fixed loop. To release the knot after it's been loaded, pull the top loop over the standing part to break the tension, then pull the running end loose. Use an extra Overhand Knot or half of a Fisherman's Bend as a backup for more important uses.

DO NOT use this knot for tying into a climbing harness. Although it does not slip under moderate loads, it can invert and fail under heavy loads, during falls, and accidental shock loading. It can also loosen when not loaded. Add the safety knot if cycled loading is expected, improving security. The Bowline is a good, useful knot but it's not meant to be a life-supporting or overhead lift knot.

 THE MOST CRUCIAL KNOTS TO KNOW

Bowline on a Bight

- Create a pair of loops at the end or mid-rope
- Easy to untie after loading
- Doesn't slip under most loads
- Emergency climbing harness

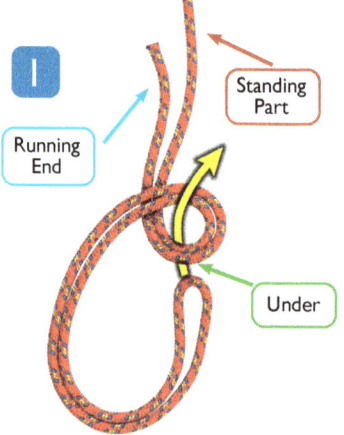

1) Create a bight at the end of the rope and create a small loop over both the standing part and running end. Pull the bight through the loop.

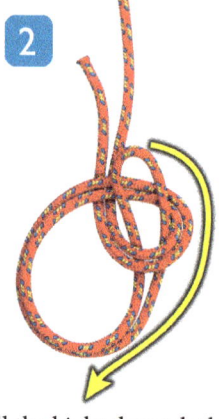

2) Pull the bight through the small loop and away from the loop. Drop the bight down over the pair of created loops.

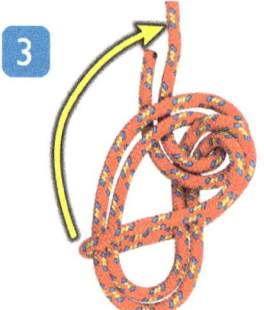

3) Raise the bight up around the two loops and behind the standing part and running end.

4) Pull down on the two loops to snug the bight behind the standing part and running end. Equalize the knot.

5) Add an Overhand Knot to the running end around the standing part for added security.

Security

Where & When to Use

The Bowline on a Bight is an excellent knot that puts two symmetric loops at the end or middle of a rope. When used as an emergency harness, make sure to have a long tail. Tie the tail end off with an Overhand Knot or half of a Double Fisherman's Bend as a safety. The structure of this knot prevents slipping. Use one loop and ignore the second loop as a solid mid-rope knot or loop.

Although this knot functions as an emergency rescue harness, even a thick 11mm line will not be comfortable for extended use around the legs. Use a commercial harness for regular climbing. This knot can also be used to create a pair of foot loops in the middle of a rope. It is also a good choice for the loop of the Trucker's Hitch, as it will not slip and is stable with side loads.

Although it will not slip under heavy loads, back up this knot with a Double Fisherman's Bend for critical applications. This knot is a much better choice than the Bowline if an important load is to be carried. In the middle of a rope, this knot is almost as effective as the Alpine Butterfly with the bonus of creating two loops as needed.

 THE MOST CRUCIAL KNOTS TO KNOW

Cat's Paw

- Easy to untie after heavy loads
- Connect a rope to a hook or loop
- Adjustable twists for rope diameter

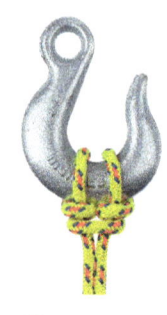

1) Create a bight at the end of the rope. Pull the bight down and over to create two loops.

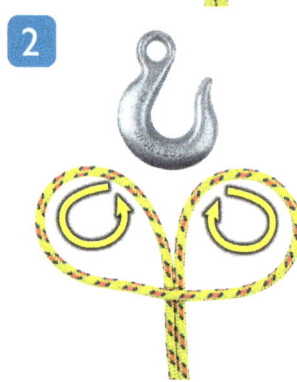

2) Twist the two loops in opposite directions. This creates twists around the standing part and running end.

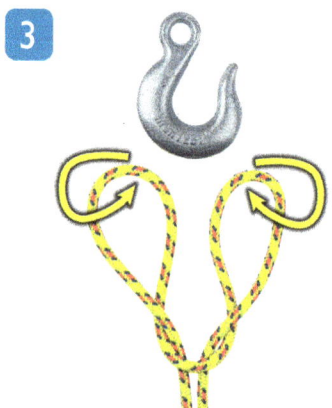

3) Repeat the twists again. Place the two loops onto a hook.

 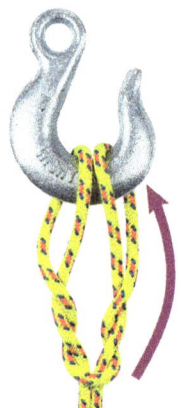

4) Pull the bottom of the loop toward the hook to tighten and dress the knot.

Where & When to Use

The Cat's Paw is based on the Lark's Head with a few extra twists to give the knot greater purchase and stability on a hook. Use this particular knot over the Lark's Head when you need extra strength or to reduce the chance of the knot slipping off an open hook, loop, or ring. This knot can also be slid onto a pole from the end to create a stronger and less slippery knot than the Lark's Head at the expense of extra time tying and dressing the knot.

This knot is useful for carrying loads on hooks with both lines pulled. One of the advantages of the knot is that if one side fails, the other side may hold long enough to safely lower the load. Do not rely on this feature, though. Consider it the backup plan.

The more either side is pulled, the more the loops shrink, gripping the hook. The Cat's Paw is an excellent choice when carrying heavy loads.

This knot does take more effort to dress and stabilize compared to the Lark's head. Either should be used with both lines tensioned. Avoid imbalance in this knot by pulling on a single side. Do not rely on this knot without an extra backup for important loads.

THE MOST CRUCIAL KNOTS TO KNOW

Cleat Hitch

- Moor a boat to a dock
- Secure a load to a mounted cleat

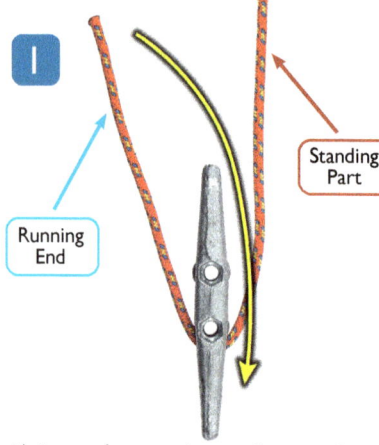

1) Loop the running end around the base of the cleat farthest away from the load (boat) and continue making a complete wrap.

2) Lay the running end over the cleat body.

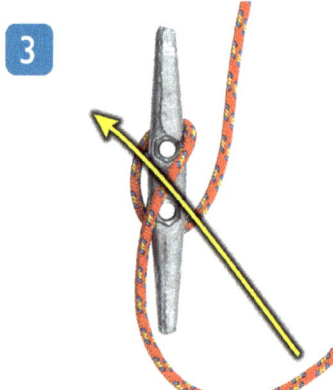

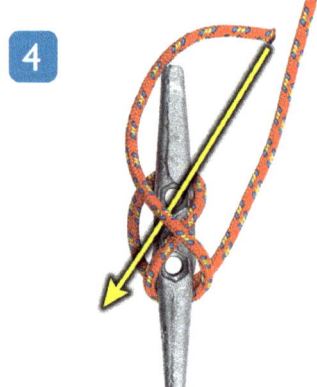

3) Loop the running end under the cleat horn and create an X with the running end.

4) Pass the running end under the other cleat horn, then thread it under the created loop, locking the knot.

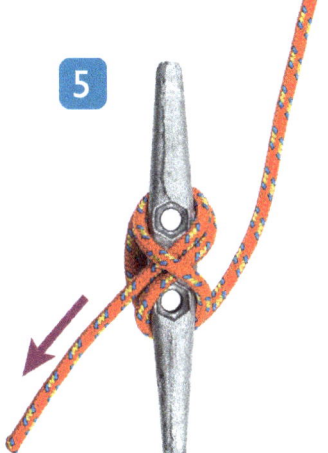

5) Dress the knot by pulling the running end taut.

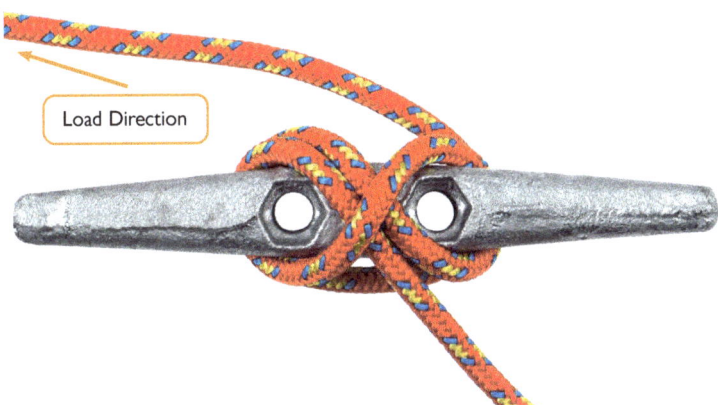

Load Direction

Where & When to Use

This is the knot for tying a boat to a dock or connecting two boats together. Tied properly, this knot can hold massive loads. The key to using this knot correctly is making sure that the standing part runs to the opposite side of the cleat from the load.

When tying large boats to a dock, do not lock the knot in Step 4. Instead, add a few more looping passes. Being able to quickly release a large boat is important for safety.

Cleats are often found in trucks and pickups, too. Using this hitch allows the user to release a load rapidly with a single hand. Even under incredible loads, the cleat hitch is easy to untie.

 THE MOST CRUCIAL KNOTS TO KNOW

Clove Hitch

- Scouting knot
- Lashing starter
- Simple to tie and inspect
- Connects to a pole or a tree
- Not good for slippery surfaces or ropes

Thread Method

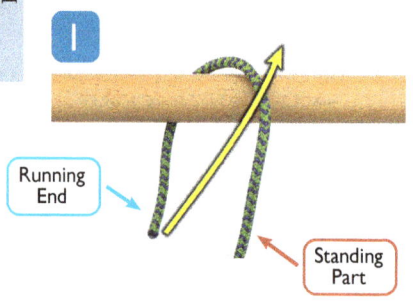

1) Loop the running end over the pole. Continue looping the running end across the standing part to create an X.

2) Wrap the running end around the pole a second time.

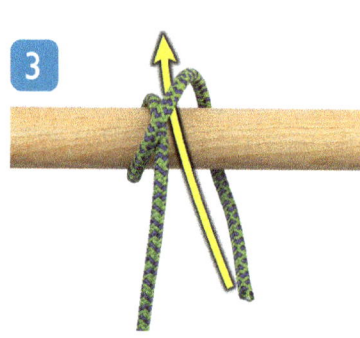

3) Pass the running end under the cross-over loop to the right of the standing part.

4) Pull the running end tight while pressing the loops together to dress the knot.

Loop Method

1) Create two loops. Make the loops over the standing part from left to right. Place the left loop over the right loop.

2) Lift both loops up and over the end of the pole.

3) Dress the knot.

Where & When to Use

The Clove Hitch is one of the Scouting knots. It is easy to tie in both the follow-through method as well as the loop method. It is the recommended starter knot for lashings to build structures with.

Be aware that the Clove Hitch is only meant for light loads or loads meant to slip. Do not use this knot by itself for important loads or where the failure of the knot will cause injury. This knot will easily slip if used on slick poles with stiff or slippery synthetic ropes.

The Constrictor Knot is a far better choice when using 550 Paracord or other slick synthetic lines for semi-permanent use. The Clove Hitch is taught as a Scouting knot instead of the Constrictor, which has more holding power. The Clove Hitch is easier to learn, tie, untie, and inspect than the Constrictor.

 The Most Crucial Knots to Know

Constrictor Knot

- Difficult to release after tensioned
- Quick-release version highly effective
- Excellent for attaching to round objects

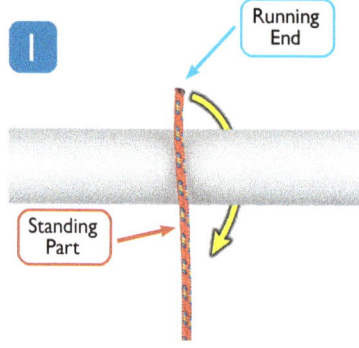

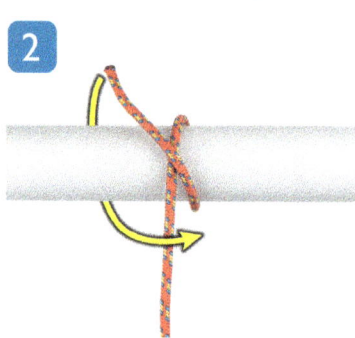

1) Loop the running end over the pole to the right of the standing part.

2) Continue wrapping the running end around the pole to create an X over the standing part. Cross the running end over the standing part.

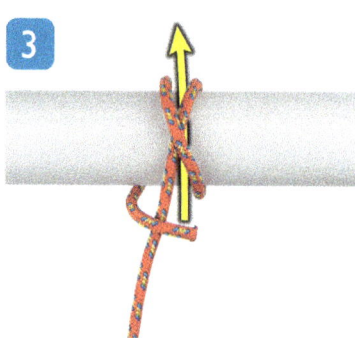

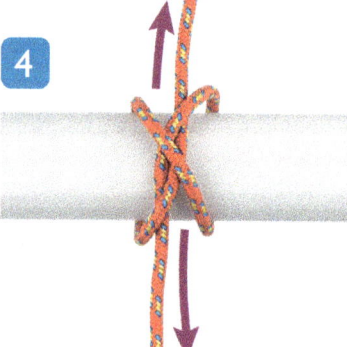

3) Pass the running end under both loops that create the X on the right-hand side of the standing part.

4) Dress the knot by pulling upward on the running end and down on the standing part. Once the knot is snug, applying additional force to the standing part tightens the Constrictor Knot even more.

5 (OPT)

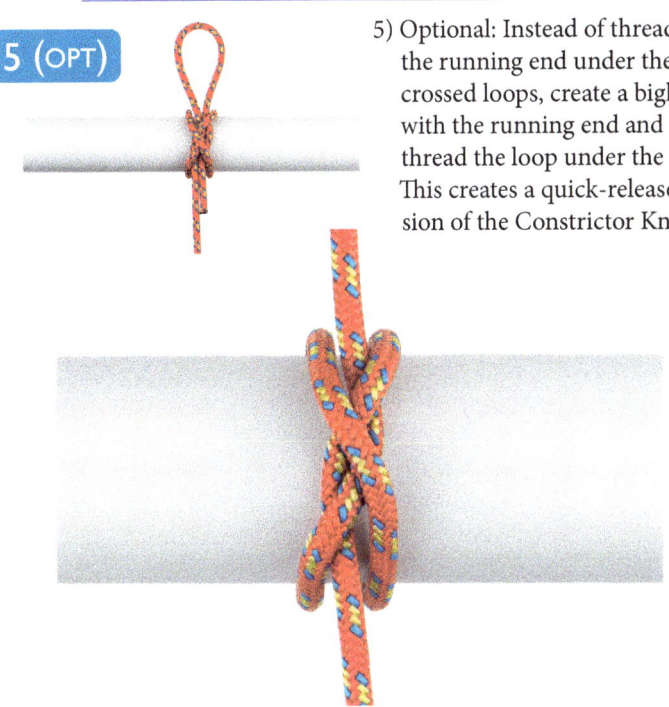

5) Optional: Instead of threading the running end under the crossed loops, create a bight with the running end and thread the loop under the X. This creates a quick-release version of the Constrictor Knot.

Where & When to Use

The Constrictor Knot is an excellent choice for tying up bags, starting a lashing on slick poles, holding a rope to prevent fraying, and even as a temporary hose or pipe clamp.

On thin line, when the Constrictor Knot is tightened or shock-loaded, it may be impossible to release without cutting the knot. Adding a bight to the running end when finishing the knot makes it easier to release. However, the release loop reduces the knot's gripping strength on some surfaces.

Note that the Constrictor Knot will slip when used on a flat surface. It's only meant to be used on round surfaces like poles and pipes. The Constrictor is more secure than the Clove Hitch for starting and ending lashings, especially with slippery rope or poles.

This knot is in the binding knot family, including the Miller's Knot, Sack Knot, Bag Knot, Strangle Knot, Clove Hitch, and the Constrictor Knot. Pay close attention to passing the running end around the standing part in Steps 2 and 3. Otherwise, you will end up tying the weaker Strangle Knot or the Clove Hitch.

The Most Crucial Knots to Know

Double Fisherman's Bend

- Easy to tie
- Extend the length of a rope
- Create a semi-permanent knot
- Extremely difficult to untie after loading

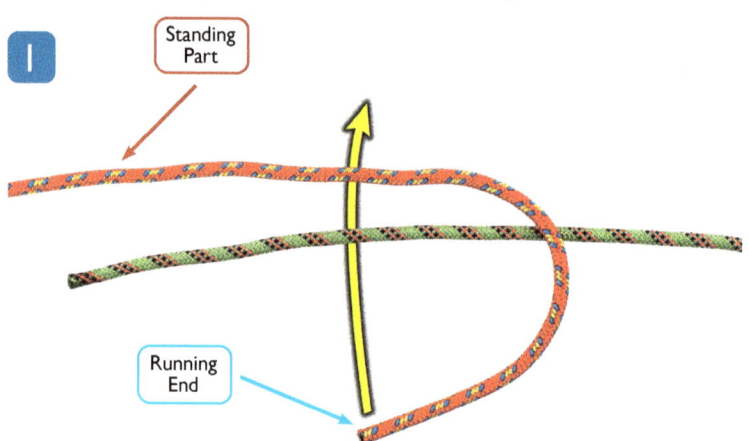

1) Loop the left line running end over the right line running end. Then, pull the left running end under both lines.

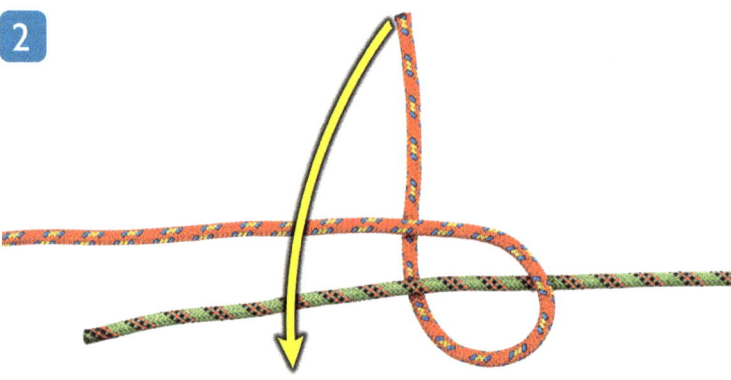

2) Wrap the left running end over both lines.

3

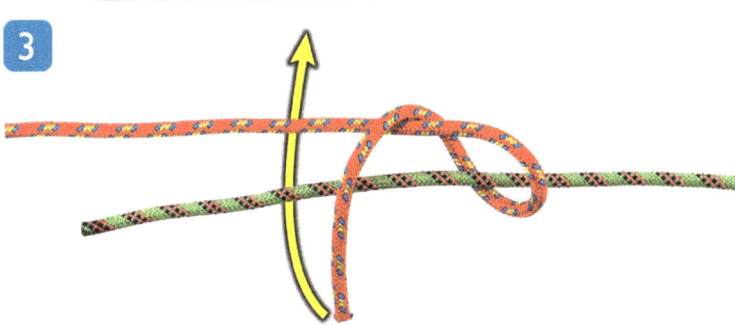

3) Wrap the left running end under the two lines again.

4

4) Place the left running end over the left standing part, then thread the left running end through the two loops, parallel to the right line.

5

5) Wrap the right running end over the left standing part. This is the repeat set of steps for the first line.

The Most Crucial Knots to Know

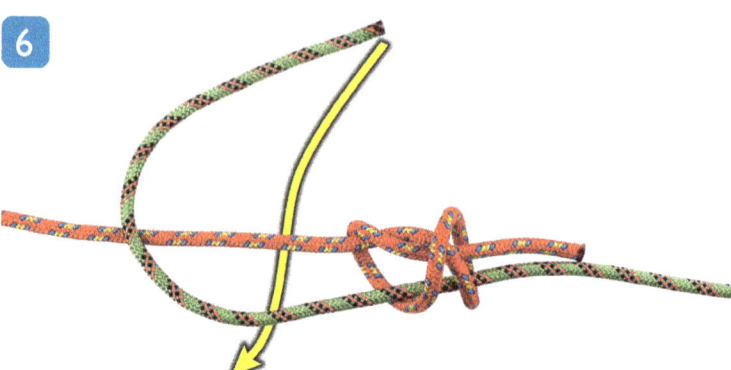

6) Wrap the right running end behind both lines.

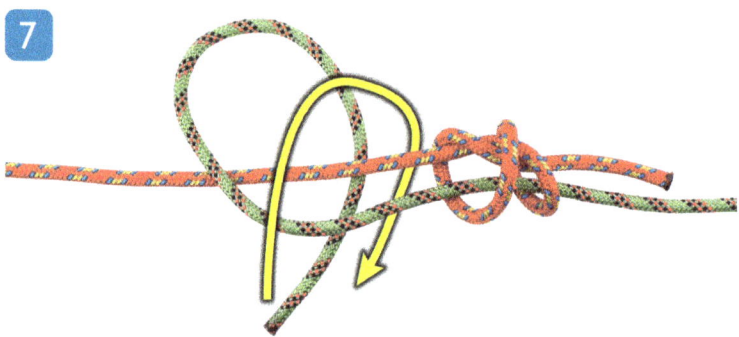

7) Wrap the right running end up, over, and behind the two lines.

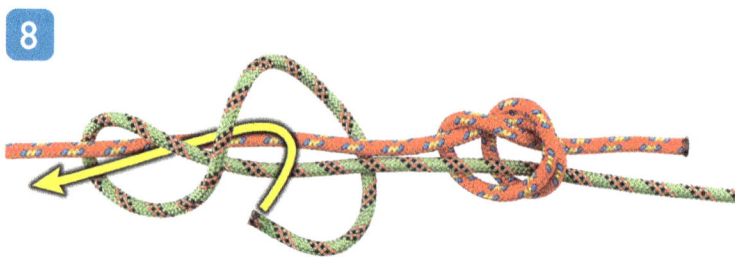

8) Place the right running end over the right standing part, then thread the right running end through the two loops, parallel to the left line.

9) Begin dressing the knot by pulling each running end tight while holding the rest of the knot.

10) Slide the knots together by pulling on the standing parts. Continue working the knot tight as the two sets of loops interlock with each other.

Where & When to Use

The Double Fisherman's Bend is an excellent choice to tie two ropes of similar diameters together. It is the knot to use when tying the Prusik Knot as a loop for attaching to a thicker line, as when climbing or ascending a fixed rope.

Inspect this knot **CAREFULLY**, especially if you have not tied it yourself when your life depends on it. It is easy to tie but it welds itself together once heavily loaded.

Other names: Grapevine Bend

 THE MOST CRUCIAL KNOTS TO KNOW

Double Overhand Stopper Knot

- Easy to tie and inspect
- Difficult to untie after loading
- Creates a moderate stopper knot

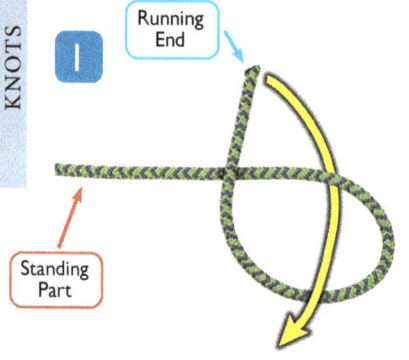

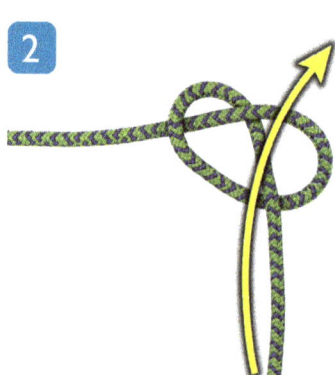

1) Start with the running end placed over the standing part to create a loop. Then, pass the running end through the loop to create an Overhand Knot.

2) Raise the running end up over the loop created to begin making another wrap around the standing part of the knot.

3) Wrap the running end around and pass it through the main loop a second time.

4) Dress the knot by pulling the running end and its loops away from the standing part. Continue working the knot until it is tightened.

Where & When to Use

The Double Overhand Stopper knot is a good choice to use when you need to prevent a rope from pulling through a hole less than twice the diameter of the rope. It is easy to learn and tie. Adding more loops does not effectively increase the thickness of the knot.

The Double Overhand Knot and the Stevedore Stopper Knot are almost interchangeable. Depending on the line quality and surface grip, the Double Overhand may be less likely to shake loose. Test both knots with your particular rope to determine which is more stable under variable conditions.

The Most Crucial Knots to Know

Figure 8 Knot

- Scouting knot
- A good, small stopper knot
- Easy to loosen once tightened
- The basis for many other knots

KNOTS

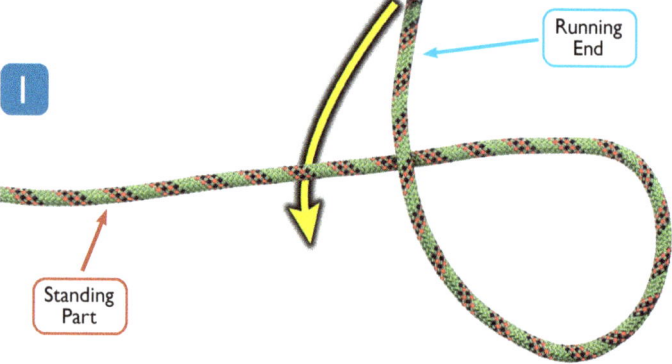

1) Start with the running end placed over the standing part. Wrap the running end around the back of the standing part.

2) Thread the running end through the loop created in the previous step.

3) Pull the running end and standing part away from each other to tighten the knot. The Figure 8 Knot will balance as it is snugged.

Where & When to Use

The Figure 8 Knot is one of the Scouting knots. This particular knot is the starting point for many of the knots contained in this book. The particular attractive symmetry of the Figure 8 makes inspection simple. If the knot does not exhibit a clear "8" shape, then the knot is tied incorrectly.

Use this knot as a simple stopper to prevent a rope from pulling through a hole. If the rope is left slack, the ease of untying this knot also means that it can loosen up and untie when loaded and unloaded multiple times. Be aware that the Double Overhand Knot and the Stevedore Knot are larger and more stable knots than the Figure 8 when used as a simple stopper.

 THE MOST CRUCIAL KNOTS TO KNOW

Figure 8 Bend (Flemish Bend)

- Connect two ropes together
- Reliable with double stopper knots
- Somewhat easy to untie after loading

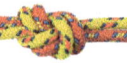

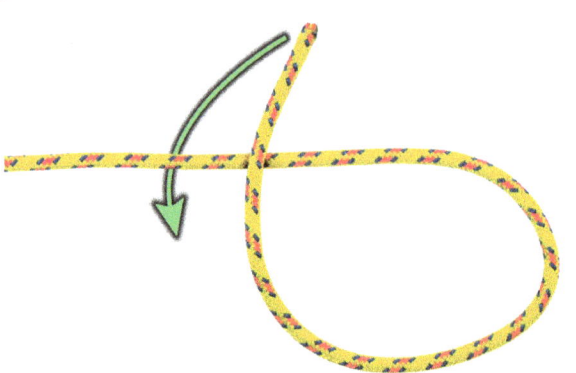

1) Start with the running end placed over the standing part of the left line. Continue looping the running end toward the standing part.

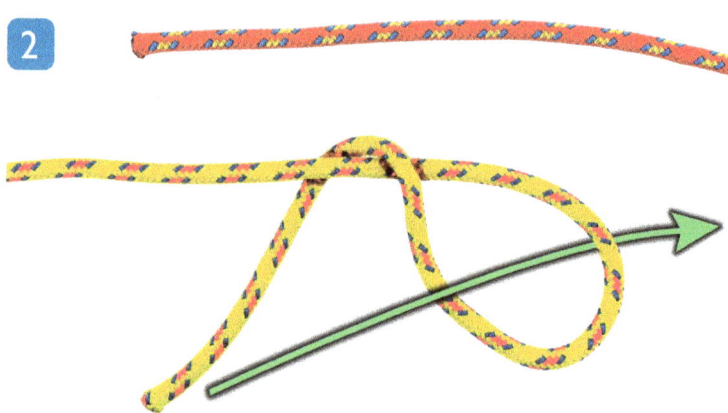

2) Pass the running end through the small loop to create the first Figure 8 knot.

3) Take the running end of the right line and thread it parallel to the running end of the left line.

4) Continue following the reverse path of the left running end.

The Most Crucial Knots to Know

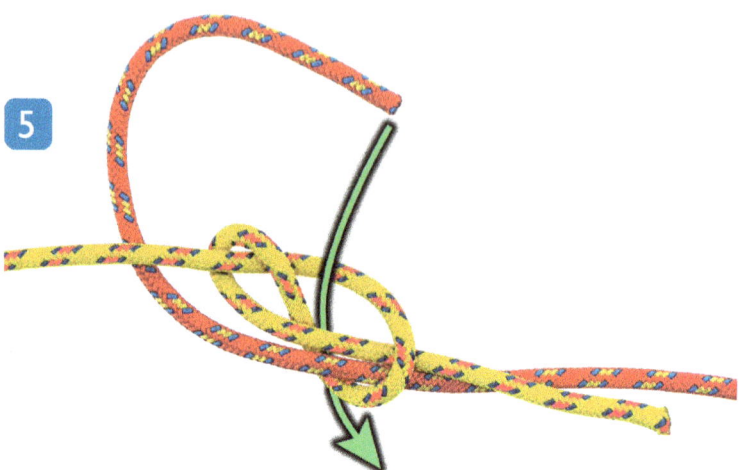

5) Continue threading the right running end along the reverse path of the left line.

6) While threading the right running end along the reverse direction of the left line, make sure to pay close attention to each loop passage.

7) Finish following the reverse path of the left line with the running end of the right line to create a symmetric knot.

 Aaron Linsdau

8) Begin dressing the knot by pulling on each of the running ends and standing parts. Ensure there are no loose loops while tightening the knot to prevent kinks. This will make the knot easier to untie later.

Where & When to Use

The Figure 8 Bend (Flemish Bend) is an excellent albeit bulky knot to tie two ropes of similar size together to extend a rope. Make sure to leave long tails and tie the tails with half of a Double Fisherman's Bend for added security when this knot is used for life support or overhead loads. It is common to leave tails that are 12-18 inches (30-46 cm).

Carefully dress this knot and balance the individual strands. If there is a loose strand in the knot, it will become incredibly difficult to untie once shock-loaded. A well-dressed Figure 8 Bend can still be a challenge to undo once it is heavily loaded while climbing.

The Most Crucial Knots to Know

Figure 8 Follow Through Loop

- Tie into a climbing harness
- Create a highly reliable loop
- Somewhat easy to untie after loading

1) Start the Figure 8 Follow Through Loop by tying a Figure 8 Knot. Leave plenty of tail in the running end. This allows for looping around the object and then allows for retracing the knot in the reverse direction.

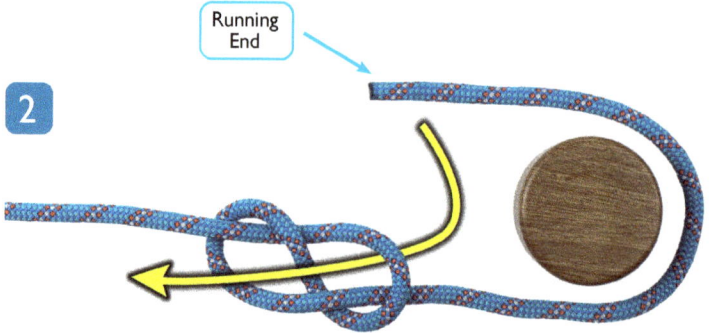

2) Pass the running end around or through the object to be tied to. Begin reverse tracing the path of the running end through the original Figure 8 Knot.

3) Loop the running end around the standing part, following the path of the original running end.

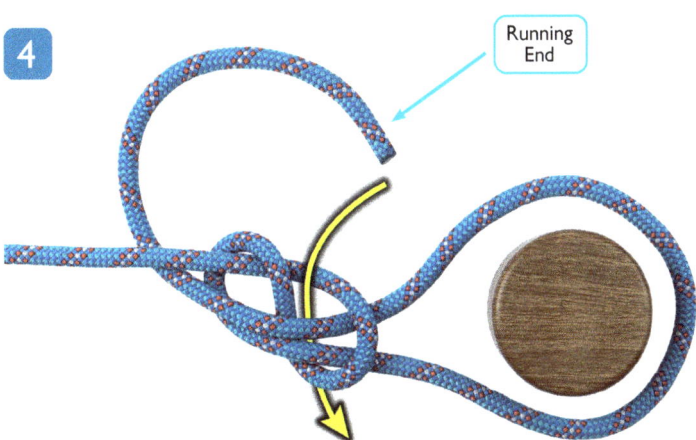

4) Pass the running end through the right-side loop of the original Figure 8 Knot. This continues the reverse tracing process.

 THE MOST CRUCIAL KNOTS TO KNOW

4

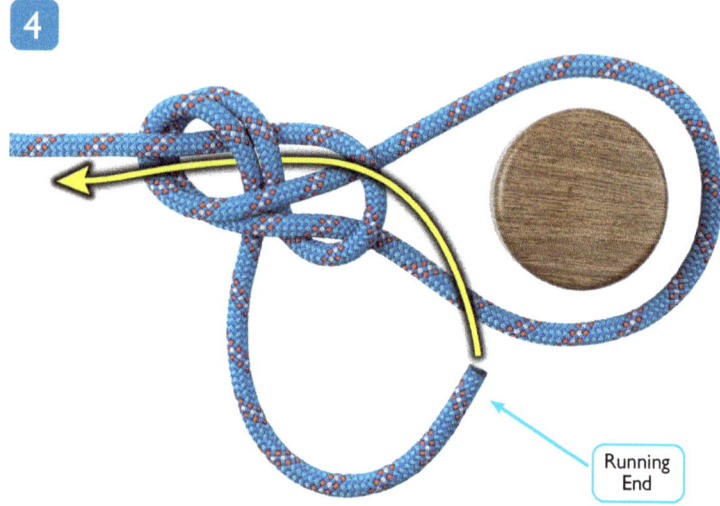

4) Finish the knot by threading the running end through the last un-doubled line, following the standing part out of the knot.

5

5) Once the knot is tied and inspected, begin dressing the knot. Take care to pull each strand individually to ensure the knot is symmetric. Avoid leaving any wide or loose loops.

6) Tie an extra Overhand Knot to prevent the running end tail from flopping around. Tie a half of a Fisherman's Bend to ensure the best security possible when used as a climbing protection. Note that most climbers use a simple Overhand Knot as the final tie-off.

Where & When to Use

The Figure 8 Follow Through Loop is the knot to tie onto a climbing harness when enjoying any type of climbing. This knot is the only generally accepted knot for climbers to protect themselves from serious or fatal falls. It is a knot that requires no additional hardware and can take massive loads.

Even with the reliability of this knot, climbers often add a safety Overhand Knot or Double Overhand Knot to the running end. This knot is added to reduce the amount of tail flailing around when climbing. It is a good additional safety measure when someone's life depends on the knot.

Carefully dress this knot and balance the individual strands. If there is a loose loop in the knot, it will become incredibly difficult to untie once shock-loaded.

The Most Crucial Knots to Know

Figure 8 on a Bight

- Easy to inspect
- Relatively easy to untie
- Create a reliable loop at the end of a rope

1) Create a bight at the end of a rope with plenty of tail. The bight becomes the running end to create the knot with.

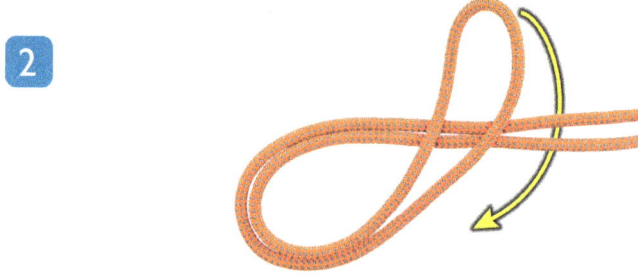

2) Lay the bight over the standing part to create a loop. Then pass the bight around the standing part.

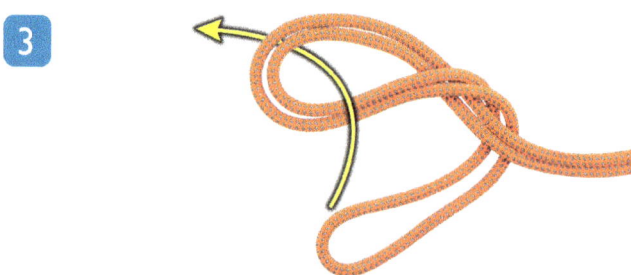

3) Pass the bight through the main loop created in the previous step.

4

4) Dress the knot by tightening each individual strand until the knot is symmetric. Avoid leaving any slack loops.

Where & When to Use

The Figure 8 on a Bight is one of the best and quickest knots to use to create a loop at the end of a rope. This knot is unlikely to slip under most loads. If the loop is meant to carry an important or life-sustaining load, finish the tail off with a Double Overhand Knot on the standing part. This will all but ensure that the knot will not come undone.

It is possible for this knot to loosen over time with cycled loading. Always inspect the knot when in use or when it has been unattended for some time.

THE MOST CRUCIAL KNOTS TO KNOW

Flat Overhand Bend

- Easy to tie
- Unlikely to become stuck
- Easy to untie when loaded

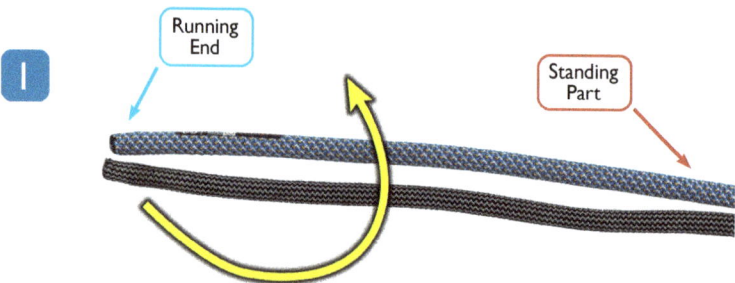

1) Lay the two lines parallel with the running ends together. Wrap both lines together over the standing part.

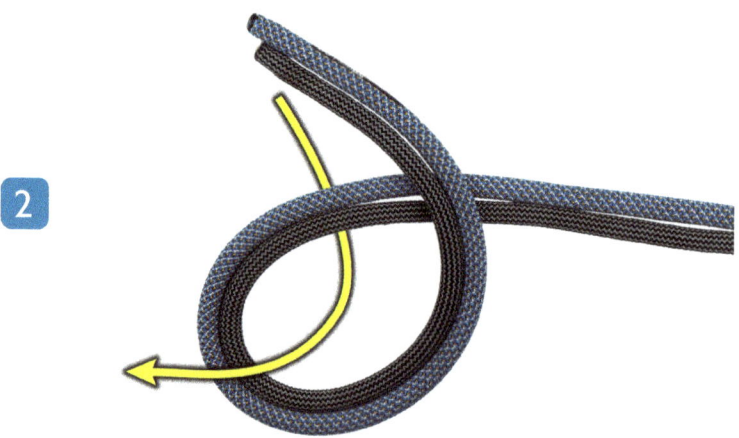

2) Wrap the running end around the standing part and thread it through the loop creating an Overhand Knot with both parallel lines.

3) Pull the standing part and running end away from each other to snug and dress the knot.

Where & When to Use

The Flat Overhand Bend is one of the easiest knots to use for connecting two ropes together. The knot is less likely to become stuck when pulling it over rough surfaces and rocks.

This knot is often used to tie two separate ropes of similar diameters to extend a rope for rappelling and retrieval. This particular knot is also referred to as the European Death Knot. With sufficiently long tails (12–18 inches / 31–46 cm), and tightened, the knot is unlikely to fail. The Double Fisherman's Bend is a safer choice but is more difficult to tie, inspect, and is difficult to untie.

NEVER use the Flat Figure 8 Bend (both ropes enter the Figure 8 on the same side) to extend a rope. It will fail under moderate loads because of the structure. Many deaths have been recorded from climbers using the Flat Figure 8 Bend to extend a rope for rappelling (abseiling).

 THE MOST CRUCIAL KNOTS TO KNOW

Girth Hitch

- Easy to tie
- Easy to untie
- Highly reliable

1) Place a bight of the strap behind the static rope.

2) Raise the opposite end of the strap to create a tighter bight. Flip the original bight over the static rope.

3) Thread the tighter bight through the original bight. Pull on the tighter bight to create the hitch.

4) Continue pulling on the bight to snug the strap.

Where & When to Use

The Girth Hitch is one of the easiest hitches to tie. This highly reliable hitch has no failure mode on its own. The only way it can fail is if the permanent loop, strap, or static rope breaks.

The hitch can be loosened and repositioned along the static rope. Once the main loop is loaded, the hitch will tighten and grip a static rope. Be aware that the Girth Hitch can slide on a smooth pole or rod. When placed on a rope, the deformation of the strap material against the rope creates surprising holding power for such a simple hitch.

The structure of this hitch is the same as the Lark's Head (Cow Hitch) but this version is tied with a fixed loop. Even when loaded and unloaded, the Girth Hitch will cinch down, holding its position on the static line.

 THE MOST CRUCIAL KNOTS TO KNOW

Highwayman's Hitch

- Quick release knot
- Carries a light to moderate load
- Holds well on irregular surfaces

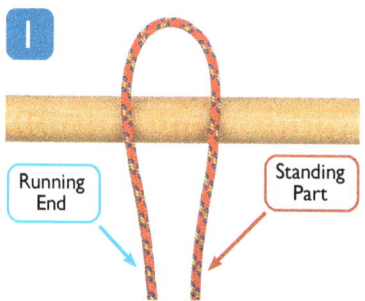

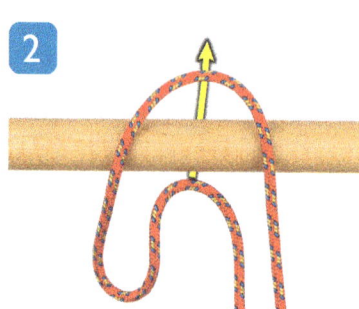

1) Create a bight at the end of the line and lay it over a pole (or over a grommet).

2) Create a second bight in the running end and place the bight under the pole (or thread it through the grommet).

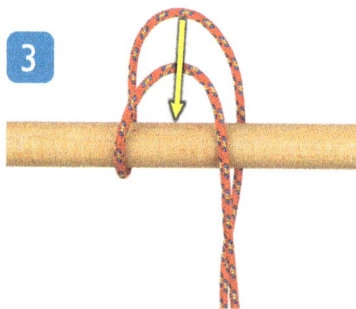

3) Lift the second bight over the original bight to wrap the original bight.

4) Pull the second bight against the surface of the pole (or grommet).

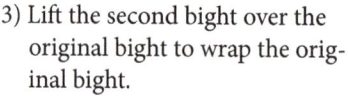

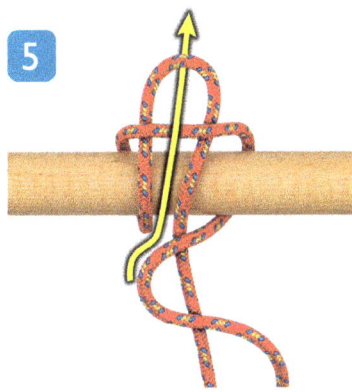

5) Create another bight with the running end and lay it over the standing part. Thread it through the first created bight.

6) Dress the knot by snugging all the loops and pulling on the standing part. Leave a large loop for more security.

WHERE & WHEN TO USE

The Highwayman's Hitch is a useful quick-release hitch to connect a line to a pole, a tarp (via a grommet), or any other object that you want the ability to release a hitch quickly. This hitch holds well with tarp grommets and rough or irregular surfaces. The Tumble Hitch, the cousin of this hitch, is better for smooth, slippery poles and slick synthetic lines than the Highwayman's Hitch.

The story about this hitch is a Highwayman (robber/criminal) would use this to tie a horse to a fixed object. They would simply pull on the running end, releasing the hitch, for a quick getaway.

 The Most Crucial Knots to Know

Honda Knot (Lariat)

- Useful for capturing
- Quick-adjusting loop
- Works well with stiff rope

1) Start with the running end laid over the standing part. Thread the running end through the loop.

2) The created Overhand Knot is used as a stopper in the Honda Knot.

3) Lay the running end with the Overhand Knot over the standing part.

4) Pass the running end through the loop to create a second, looser overhand knot.

5) Pull the running end far enough out to create another loop.

6) Pass the running end through the loop of the second Overhand Knot.

7) Tighten the second Overhand Knot, then expand the small loop until the first Overhand Knot locks to the second. Then either create a bight in the standing part and loop it through the small loop or take the standing part and thread it through the fixed loop.

8) Adjust the capture loop as necessary. The holding loop is shown as overly large for the illustration. In practice, the holding loop is made smaller to control the flow of the capture loop.

Where & When to Use

The Honda Knot (Lariat) is the knot to use when you need a slippery loop that will rapidly constrict yet will loosen the moment tension is released on the standing part. Adjusting the holding loop size allows for control of how the main loop performs.

Lariat rope is stiff and often has a manufactured, crimped, or spliced capture loop from the manufacturer. Stiff rope is good for active capture of animals but a flexible line is perfect for capturing small animals in snares. Be aware that as long as there is tension on the standing part of the line, there is the potential for choking whatever is captured.

 THE MOST CRUCIAL KNOTS TO KNOW

Improved Clinch Knot

- An important fishing knot
- Holds high loads without slipping
- Perfect for tying slippery monofilament to a hook

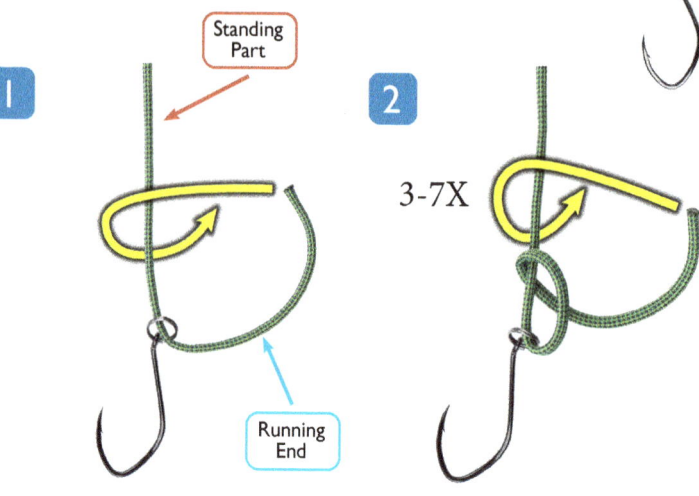

1) Thread the running end through the eye of the hook. Start wrapping the running end around the standing part while holding onto the hook so it doesn't spin.

2) Loop the running end around the standing part 3 to 7 times.

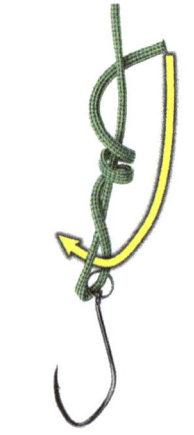

3) Thread the running end through the loop attached to the eye of the hook.

4) Thread the running end through the loop created in Step 3.

5) Dress the knot by wetting the loops and pulling on the standing part while holding onto the hook.

Where & When to Use

If there is one knot to learn as an angler, the Improved Clinch Knot is it. Most anglers will use this singular knot to tie monofilament line to a hook for their entire lives and learn nothing else. It is reliable and relatively easy to tie.

When tightening monofilament, moisten the line first to lubricate it. The knot changes structure while tightening. The tension will create neat, symmetric loops. Clip off the extra tag end on the running end.

The Improved Clinch Knot provides an extra amount of grip over the traditional Clinch Knot to prevent slipping. The disadvantage to the improved version is the increased chance of the end of the knot snagging on fine-edged underwater obstacles.

 The Most Crucial Knots to Know

Lark's Head (Cow Hitch)

- Easy to untie
- Unlikely to bind
- Good option to the Clove Hitch

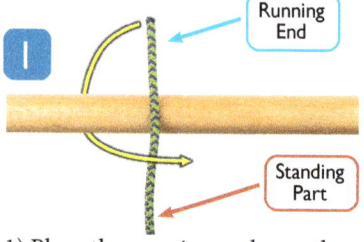

1) Place the running end over the object. Wrap the running end around the object and then in front of the standing part.

2) Wrap the running end behind the object.

3) Wrap the running end over the object and thread it between the object and the front loop.

4) Dress the knot by snugging each of the loops.

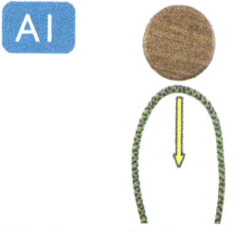

A1) Create a bight in the rope. Pull the bight downward over the standing part.

A2) The two created loops are now in opposition to each other and are ready for the next step.

A3) Fold one loop onto the other.

A4) Place the loop pair over the object to be hitched to.

Where & When to Use

The Lark's Head (Cow Hitch) is the same knot as the Girth Hitch. When tied with a running end, this hitch is fast and easy to learn but is to be used for non-critical applications. If let slack and rotated on smooth objects with a slippery rope, the Lark's Head can come undone even with long tails.

The alternate tying method (A1-A4) is a fast tying option. When the object has an end to be looped over, this is the fastest method.

When tied with a permanent loop (Girth Hitch) at the end of the rope or in the middle of a strap, there is essentially no chance for the knot to fail. This mode of the knot is highly reliable but requires a permanent strong loop. It will not fail as long as the rope or strap does not break.

 THE MOST CRUCIAL KNOTS TO KNOW

Marlinspike Hitch

- Connect a series of objects
- Create an emergency ladder
- Quickly connect a rope to an object

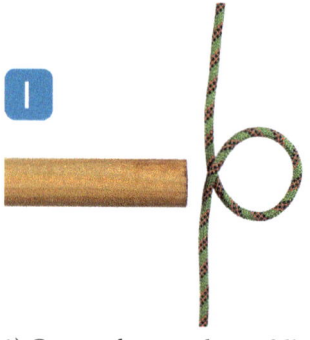

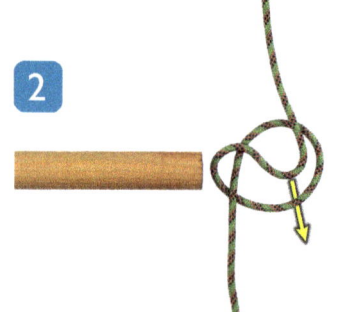

1) Create a loop in the middle of a rope.

2) Create a bight in the rope that is under the loop and pull it through the first loop.

3) Slide the object into the main loop. This is the same knot as the Slip Knot with an object passed through the main sliding loop.

4) Add a sequence of hitches to create a ladder or connect a series of objects. Note the reversing of how the hitch is tied on either side. This is not critical to the stability of the hitch but rather illustrates how it can be tied left or right-handed.

Where & When to Use

The Marlinspike Hitch is the same knot as the Slip Knot but attached to an object. By placing the object or pole through the adjustable loop, a sequence of objects can be tied to a single rope.

To create an impromptu ladder using this knot sequence safely, the ends of the spars or poles must have bulbs on them to prevent the rope from slipping off. Once tensioned and loaded, the knots stay in place surprisingly well with flexible line.

Another use of this knot is to quickly tie to any object in the middle of the line. The end of the object must be accessible to slip the Marlinspike Hitch over.

 THE MOST CRUCIAL KNOTS TO KNOW

Miller's Knot

- Tie a bag closed
- Bundle items (Sticks)
- Bind a rolled item (Blanket)

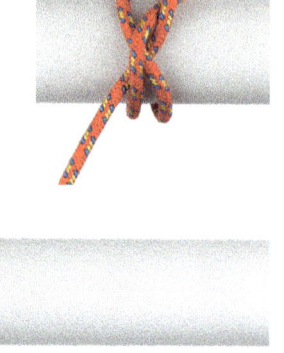

1) Place the running end over the object. Then, wrap the running end around the object.

2) Wrap the running end around the front of the object and over the standing part.

3) Wrap the running end around the object a second time, laying the line parallel to the first full wrap. Then, thread the running end between the standing part and the object.

4) Dress the knot by pulling on the standing part.

Where & When to Use

The Miller's Knot is in the family of binding loops including the Constrictor Knot, Sack Knot, Clove Hitch, Bag Knot, and Strangle Knot. Each of these knots is a variation on the other. The Constrictor has the strongest ratcheting action but is also the most difficult to remove. The Miller's Knot is easier to pull apart.

To make the Miller's Knot easier to undo, create a bight at on the running end and pass that bight under the standing part in Step 3.

 THE MOST CRUCIAL KNOTS TO KNOW

Mooring Hitch

- Strong and versatile
- Quick-release under tension
- Easy to tie in difficult conditions

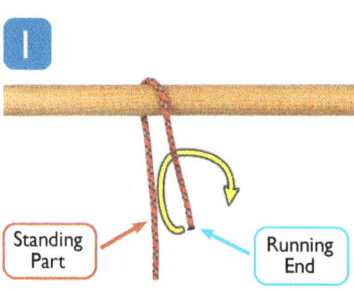

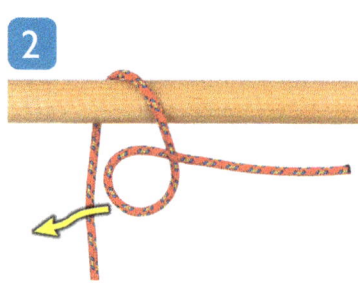

1) Loop the running end over a pole or around the object to be tied to.

2) Create a loop with the running end and lay the loop over the running end.

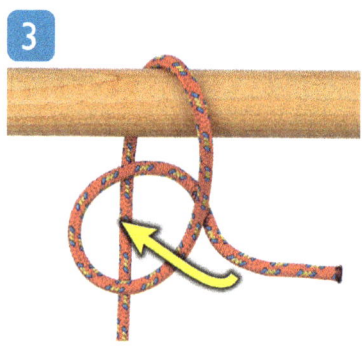

3) Create a bight in the running end. Begin pulling the bight over the loop created in the previous step.

4) Pull the bight on the running end under the standing part and then back over the loop created in the first steps.

Aaron Linsdau

5

5) Dress the knot by pulling on the standing part while holding the running end bight. Continue snugging the lines until the knot is tight.

Where & When to Use

The Mooring Hitch is best used when tying to something that needs to be easily released. With a sufficiently long loop and tail in the standing part, the knot is strong and stable.

This knot combined with the Two Half-Hitches on the other end of the rope is an excellent choice for tying down light to medium loads. This knot is also used for boating when a strong connection is required while still allowing for rapid release.

This knot will not hold its position if enough tension is applied to the standing part. If position and adjustability are important, use the Taut-Line Hitch with a quick-release loop.

 THE MOST CRUCIAL KNOTS TO KNOW

Munter Hitch

- Automatically changes direction
- Create a belay without an aid device
- Requires only one carabiner for belay

KNOTS

1) Start with a climbing rope and large climbing carabiner.

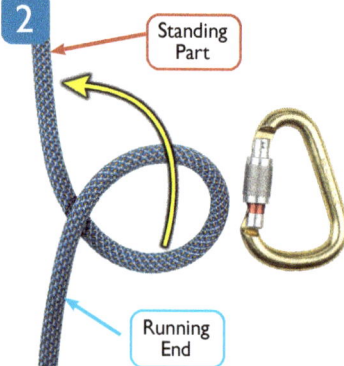

2) Create a single loop. Then, fold the lower loop toward the standing part.

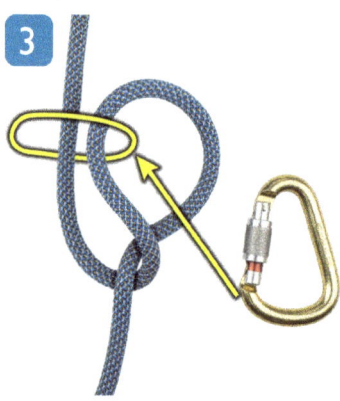

3) Clip the carabiner to the loop and standing part.

4) Clip the carabiner to a climbing harness at the proper attachment point and lock the carabiner.

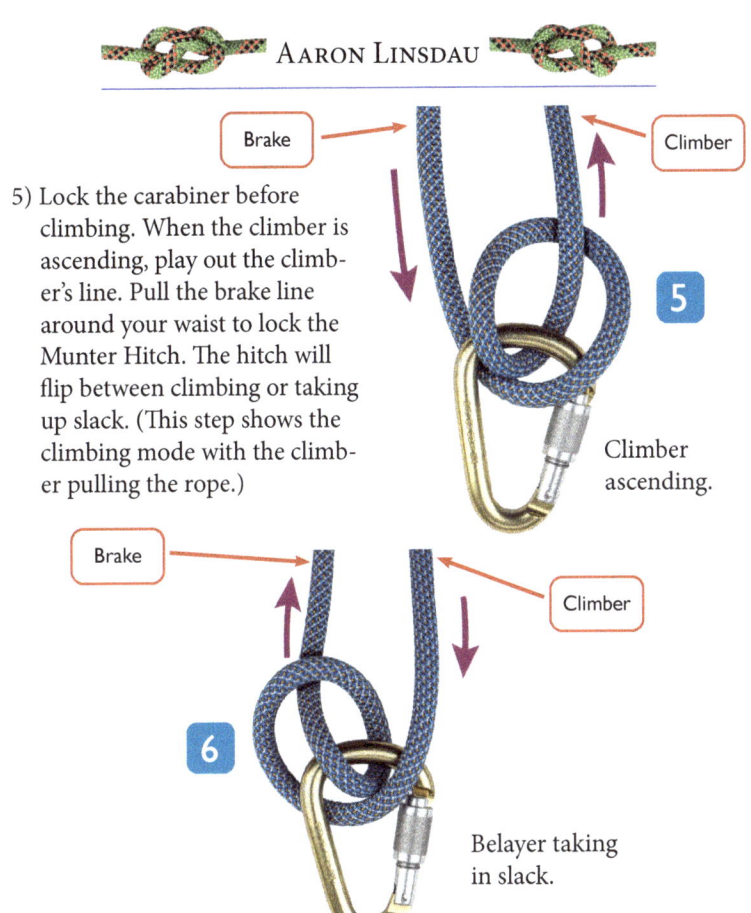

5) Lock the carabiner before climbing. When the climber is ascending, play out the climber's line. Pull the brake line around your waist to lock the Munter Hitch. The hitch will flip between climbing or taking up slack. (This step shows the climbing mode with the climber pulling the rope.)

Climber ascending.

Belayer taking in slack.

6) When taking up slack, pull on the brake hand line. The hitch will flip through the carabiner. This allows the belayer to pull rope back through the hitch and carabiner.

Where & When to Use

The Munter Hitch is an excellent option to belay a climber when a climbing aid (Grigri, ATC, Figure 8, etc.) is unavailable. The hitch is easy to inspect and works well. It will take high loads from significant falls with little effort.

ONLY use a locking carabiner for this hitch. It is easy to open the gate accidentally when belaying with this hitch, especially using popular wire gate carabiners. Also, use a wide or pear locking carabiner. A small D-shaped carabiner will not work well because the hitch may fail to flip through the carabiner. It can snag on a wire or non-locking gate, releasing the rope, causing an accident.

 THE MOST CRUCIAL KNOTS TO KNOW

Overhand Bight

- Easy to inspect
- Easiest knot to create a loop
- Difficult to untie once loaded

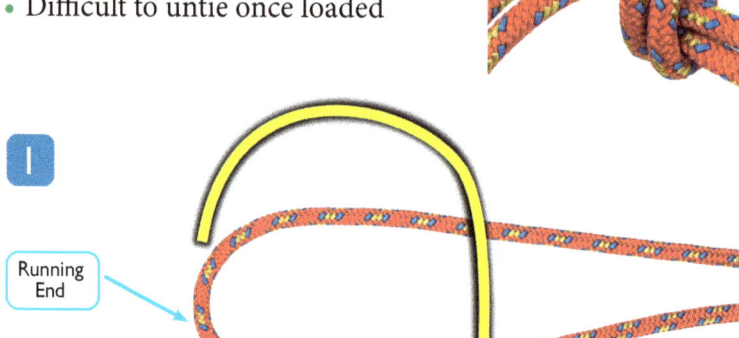

1) Create a bight at the end of the rope, leaving enough to tie the knot with. Then, loop the bight over the created standing part of the rope.

2) Once the bight is laid over the standing part, thread the bight through the created loop.

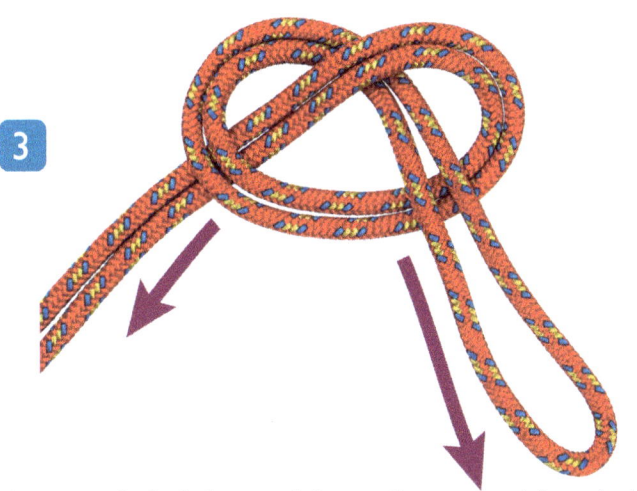

3) Tension the bight loop and the standing part to tighten the knot. Make sure there are no loose loops or lines.

Where & When to Use

The Overhand Bight is the simplest knot to create a loop at the end of a rope with. This knot is strong and is easy to inspect, making it versatile and valuable. If used for carrying important loads, add an additional Overhand Knot or half of a Double Fisherman's Bend to the free end of the line.

If this loop is to take a heavy load, make sure to leave plenty of tail for safety. This knot will bind up and is difficult to untie once shock-loaded. It is easier to tie than the Figure Eight on a Bight.

 The Most Crucial Knots to Know

Overhand Knot (Half Hitch)

- Easiest knot to tie
- Light-duty stopper knot
- Starter for more complex knots

1) Create a loop with the running end by laying the running end over the standing part.

2) Wrap the running end around the standing part and thread it through the loop.

1) To create the Half Hitch, wrap the running end around the object, then wrap the running end around the standing part and pass it through the created loop.

2) Dress the knot by pulling on the standing part and running end to tighten the hitch against the object.

Where & When to Use

The Overhand Knot is the simplest knot to tie. The Overhand Knot creates a small stopper knot that is easily untied in most ropes. This knot is the basis or completion knot for many more complex knots and hitches.

In addition, the Half Hitch is the easiest hitch to tie. It is the basis for the Two Half-Hitches, the Taut-Line Hitch, and many other loop and attachment hitches. This is a light-duty hitch meant only to hold minor loads.

 THE MOST CRUCIAL KNOTS TO KNOW

Palomar Knot

- Strong and compact
- Works well with braided line
- Easy to tie in rough conditions

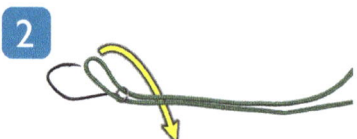

1) Create a bight in the line with enough tail to complete the knot. Thread the bight through the eye of the hook.

2) Loop the bight around and behind the standing part.

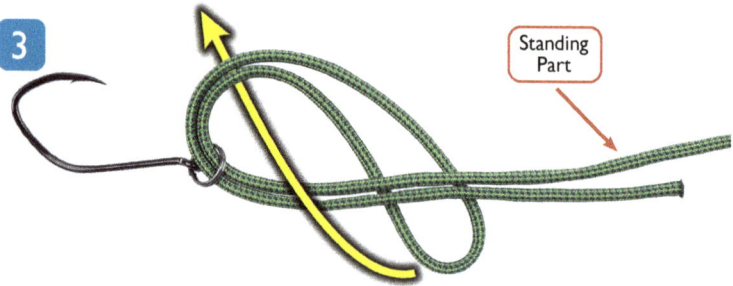

3) Continue looping the bight around the standing part. Thread it through the created loop which will result in an Overhand Knot.

4) Loop the bight over the hook and pull it around toward the eye of the hook.

5) Continue pulling the bight past the eye of the hook and over the standing part.

6) Moisten the body of the knot. Pull the standing part and the tail away from the knot. The knot will tighten and change structure until it binds on it itself. Clip the tail to minimize snagging and visibility.

Where & When to Use

The Palomar Knot is one of the easiest fishing knots to tie, especially under difficult fishing and weather conditions. This knot is similar in strength to the Improved Clinch Knot, depending on the testing method and fishing anecdotes.

One disadvantage to the Palomar Knot is the requirement for the bight loop to be larger than the lure. This may influence some anglers in their preference. The simplicity of tying the Palomar compared to other fishing knots makes it attractive for rough conditions. The knot works with monofilament and fluorocarbon lines. Braided line may take more effort to tie with this knot depending on the brand.

 THE MOST CRUCIAL KNOTS TO KNOW

Pipe Hitch

- Pull stakes out of the ground
- Lift a smooth cylindrical object
- Connect a rope to a smooth pipe

1) Begin wrapping the running end around the pipe.

2) Wrap the rope at least four times around the pipe. Add more loops if needed to increase friction to prevent slipping.

Two Half-Hitches

3) Finish off the Pipe Hitch by using the running end to tie a Two Half-Hitches to the standing part.

4) Create a loop with the standing part to guide the lifting force. Make sure the standing part goes over the loop and not under it, otherwise the loop will slip. The pulling force will press the loop against the pipe.

Where & When to Use

The Pipe Hitch is self-binding, so it does very well with synthetic rope on smooth, cylindrical surfaces. It is also excellent for pulling stuck wooden tent stakes out of the ground or lifting logs.

If the turns of the hitch slip, simply add more turns. Eventually, the wrap friction becomes high enough that the hitch will not slide.

The Pipe Hitch can also be tied using a continuous loop of rope or webbing. Start with a bight (running end) and wrap at least four times, then thread the bight up through the starting loop. This is an excellent variation to use for pulling stuck tent stakes, as the loop makes it easier to pull on the stake. Use a medium diameter rope for the best friction and holding power.

 THE MOST CRUCIAL KNOTS TO KNOW

Prusik Knot

- Connect to a static line
- Useful for climbing and rescue
- Easily adjusted and repositioned

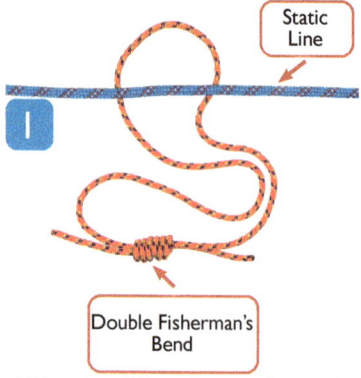

1) Tie a Double Fisherman's Bend to create a loop for the Prusik Knot. Lay it behind the static line to start.

2) Wrap the Prusik line around the static line to create a Girth Hitch.

3) Repeat the process of threading the main loop through the Girth Hitch loop again.

4) Repeat Step 3 one more time.

5) Once there are three turns, tighten the loops and make them symmetric and neat to dress the knot.

6) Release tension on the knot, grip the Prusik Knot loops, and slide it up or down the static line to make an ascent.

Where & When to Use

The Prusik Knot is one of the fundamental climbing and rescue knots. It is often used as a backup to mechanical ascenders while ascending a static line attached to a cliff or mountain.

This knot is also used in the Texas Prusik to ascend a static line with only an accessory cord. Use this ascending method as a fallback plan when mechanical ascenders are unavailable.

The Klemheist and Bachmann Knots are variations on the Prusik that can be valuable to learn as well.

The Most Crucial Knots to Know

San Diego Jam Knot

- Strong and reliable
- Works well with all line types
- Connect a hook to a fishing line

1) Thread the running end through the eye of the hook. Start wrapping the running end around the standing part while holding onto the hook so it doesn't spin.

2) Create a series of wraps with the running end toward the hook, keeping the wraps fairly tight.

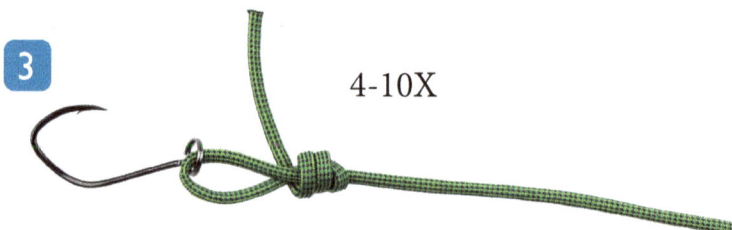

4-10X

3) For lighter lines, use additional wraps. If using a 40-pound line or heavier, 3-4 turns are usually effective. If using a 6- to 10-pound line, use 8-10 turns to give the knot enough holding power.

4) Thread the running end through the loop attached to the eye of the hook.

5) Thread the running end through the first wrapping loop, farthest away from the eye of the hook.

6) Moisten the knot and begin pulling on the standing part while holding the running end to prevent the knot from spinning apart. Keep the loops symmetric and prevent overlap. Snip the excess tag on the running end.

Where & When to Use

The San Diego Jam Knot was developed during the era of the famous San Diego tuna fishing fleet. This knot has nearly the same strength as the line that it is used with, virtually eliminating the likelihood of losing a fish or hook due to knot failure.

This knot works well with monofilament, fluorocarbon, and braided fishing lines. When tightening, make sure the loops stay symmetric. Avoid allowing the loops to overlap each other.

Note that the thinner the line, the more turns are required to complete the knot. With lines of 40+ pounds, the 3 turns shown are adequate. With 10 pound line, use 8 turns to create enough friction for the knot to hold.

The Most Crucial Knots to Know

Sheet Bend

- Scouting Knot
- Tie two ropes together
- Useful for different diameter lines

1) Create a bight in the larger of the two lines (green line). Place the running end of the thinner line (orange line) behind the bight of the larger line.

2) Wrap the running end of the thinner line around the top of the standing part of the larger line. Continue wrapping the thinner running end behind the running end of the thicker line.

3) Wrap the running end of the thinner line over the running end of the larger line. Continue by threading the running end of the thinner line between the standing parts of both lines.

4) Dress the knot by holding both parts of the thicker line and pulling on the running end of the thinner line.

5) Optional: To make the knot more secure, made a second turn of the running end of the thinner line.

Where & When to Use

The Sheet Bend is one of the fundamental Scouting knots and is useful for extending a rope by tying two ropes together. It is also helpful for connecting two ropes of dissimilar diameters. The thicker rope should be the one with the starting bight (green in the illustrations). Use the thinner rope to create the knot with (orange in the illustrations).

Note that the Sheet Bend can loosen over time when the rope is slacked and tightened multiple times. The best method for adding more security is to add the second inner loop with the thinner line.

 THE MOST CRUCIAL KNOTS TO KNOW

Shoelace Bow

- Easy to tie
- Easy to untie
- Common shoe lacing knot

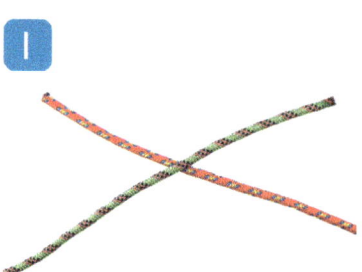

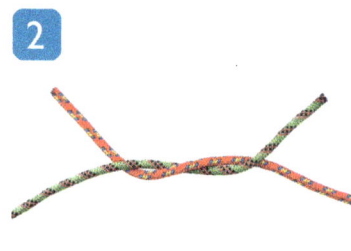

1) Cross the right and left lines.

2) Wrap the right line around the left line, creating an open Overhand Knot.

3) Create bights in both lines.

4) Cross the right bight over the left bight.

5

5) Pass the bights of both lines through the main opening in the same fashion as the Square Knot. Pull on both bights to tighten and secure the knot.

Where & When to Use

The Shoelace Bow is a Square Knot made with bights after an open Overhand Knot is made with the two lines. This is the most common knot used by people around the world. From basic tennis shoes to high-end mountaineering boots, the lowly Shoelace Knot is what keeps shoes on people's feet.

In order to make the knot more secure, take the two bight loops and tie an additional overhand knot. This essentially creates a stacked Square Knot. This method is effective with slippery laces or ones that repeatedly come untied from snagging or shoe flexing.

 THE MOST CRUCIAL KNOTS TO KNOW

Siberian Hitch (Packer's Knot)

- Quick-release knot
- Easy to tie with mittens in the cold
- Excellent for a survival tarp grommet knot

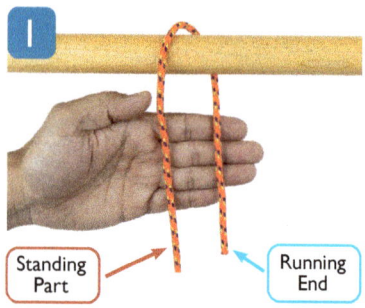

1) Wrap the standing part around the object to be tied to (pole, tarp grommet, etc.). Place your hand behind both the standing part and running end.

2) Wrap the running end behind your hand. Pull the running end over the top of your hand and in front of both lines.

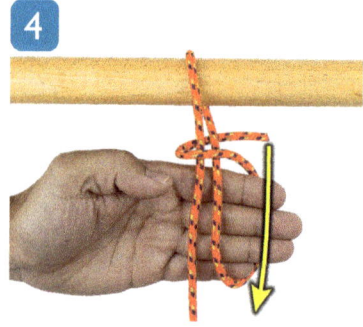

3) Wrap the running end behind both lines looped around (or through) the object.

4) Pull the running end over your hand so there is enough line to create a large loop in the next sequence of steps.

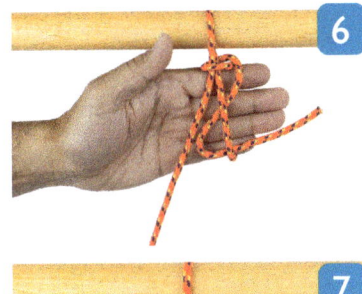
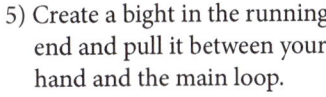

5) Create a bight in the running end and pull it between your hand and the main loop.

6) While holding the running end bight with your right hand, remove your left hand from the loops.

7) Pull the bight on the running end until the knot is tight.

Where & When to Use

The Siberian Hitch (Packer's Knot) is an excellent choice for a quick-release knot when tying a line to a tarp survival shelter. Loop the line through the grommet and then tie this knot. The quick-release feature allows the rapid untying of the knot no matter how much tension is on the standing part. The knot doesn't bind up under load. However, the knot slides and cannot hold its position like the Taut-Line Hitch.

Make sure to create a large release loop and leave plenty of running end when this knot is going to be left unattended. This knot is essentially a Figure 8 Knot with a release bight and the standing part threaded through the first loop.

 THE MOST CRUCIAL KNOTS TO KNOW

Slip Knot

- Easy to tie
- Easy to untie
- Slides under light loads

1) Create a loop with the running end over the standing part.

2) Create a bight in the standing part. Thread the bight through the loop over the standing part.

3) Pull on the running end and main loop to tighten and dress the knot.

Where & When to Use

The Slip Knot is one of the easiest sliding loop knots to tie. It can be tied in the middle of a rope, making it highly versatile. Once the loop fully constricts around a hard object, the knot remains easy to release and does not bind. On a compressible surface, it constricts well while remaining easy to release.

There is one instance where the running end is used for the slipping loop. When using the Slip Knot for the Trucker's Hitch, create a bight as shown in Steps 2 and 3 with the running end instead. Using the standing part for the main loop will cause the Trucker's Hitch to collapse.

 THE MOST CRUCIAL KNOTS TO KNOW

Square Knot

- Scouting knot
- Best tied against a surface
- Best with similar-diamenter ropes

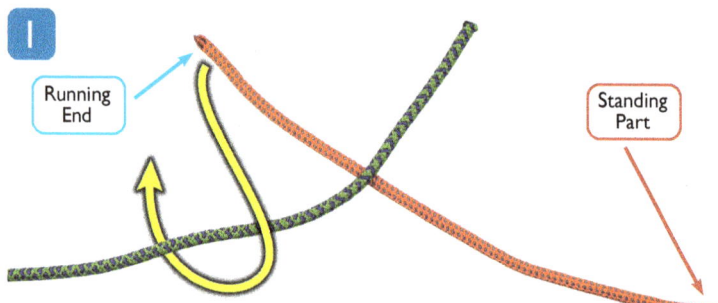

1) Place the right line (orange) running end behind the running end of the left line (green). Then, wrap the running end around the standing part of the left line.

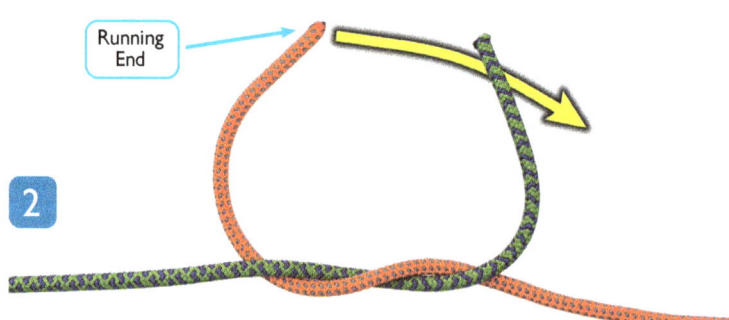

2) Take the running end of the right line and place it behind the running end of the left line.

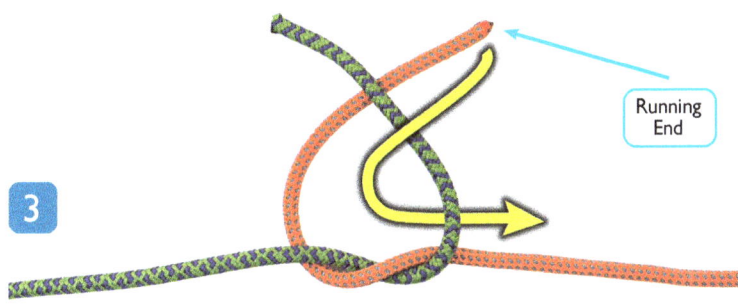

3) Continue with the right running end and wrap it over and through the loop created with the left running end.

Where & When to Use

The Square Knot is one of the fundamental Scouting knots. It is an excellent choice for connecting two ropes under certain conditions. It requires constant tension or pressure to stay tied with stiff ropes. It may fall apart under cycled loading. It works well with ropes, straps, and cloth that is rough or flexible.

The Square Knot is best used when it is placed against something rather than floating in the air by itself. Examples of placing the Square Knot against a surface are: tying string around a box, tying an umbrella with built-in straps, and tying a bandanna around your head or neck. This knot is also used in first aid situations for tying bandages..

 THE MOST CRUCIAL KNOTS TO KNOW

Stevedore Stopper Knot

- Easy to untie
- Stable stopper knot
- Strong mid-sized stopper knot

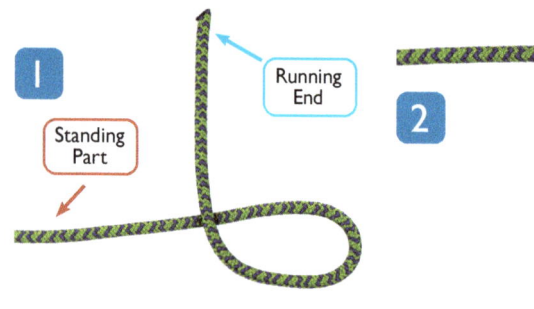

1) Create a loop by laying the running end on the standing part.

2) Wrap the running end around the standing part.

3) Continue wrapping the running end over the loop.

4) Thread the running end through the main loop.

5) Pull on both the running end and the standing part to dress the knot.

Where & When to Use

The Stevedore Stopper Knot is a moderately bulky stopper knot. It is highly effective at preventing a line from pulling through a constricted hole such as a grommet on a tarp.

The Stevedore Stopper Knot and the Double Overhand Knot are almost interchangeable. Depending on the line quality and surface grip, the Double Overhand may be less likely to shake loose. Test both knots with your particular rope to determine which is more stable under variable conditions.

 THE MOST CRUCIAL KNOTS TO KNOW

Taut-Line Hitch

- Scouting knot
- Tent guyline tensioning
- Excellent holding power

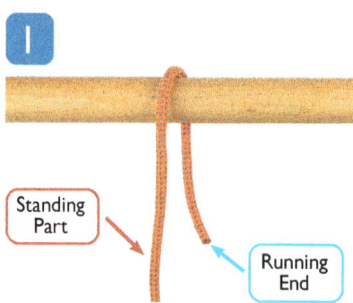

1) Wrap the running end of the line behind the object or through a grommet, tie-down loop, etc.

2) Loop the running end around the standing part and thread it through the created loop.

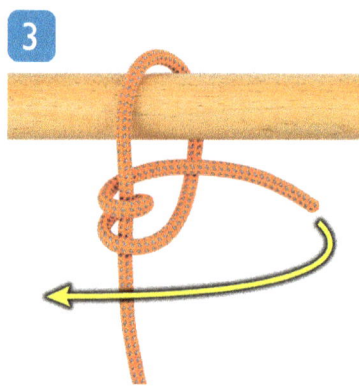

3) Create a second wrap inside the main loop on the standing part. Then, fold the running end over the standing part.

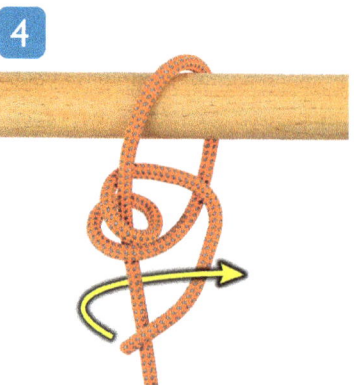

4) Thread the running end through the loop created in Step 3.

5) Dress the knot by snugging up all of the loops and pull on the running end to finish tightening the hitch.

Where & When to Use

The Taut-Line Hitch is one of the fundamental Scouting knots. This hitch is the knot to use on thin guylines for tents and tarps. Once tightened, the knot stays in position under a consistent load.

If the load is variable, as in windy conditions with a tent, this hitch may slip. Normally, the hitch will only slide a little until the line is slightly loose and then holds its position. With thin guylines, this hitch is highly reliable.

This knot does not stay together well when made with stiff, large-diameter rope and accessory cords. It does work well with flexible braided rope of thin and moderate diameters.

 THE MOST CRUCIAL KNOTS TO KNOW

Timber Hitch

- Easy to tie
- Easy to untie
- Does not bind
- Grips rough surfaces

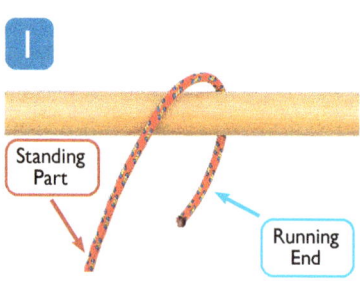

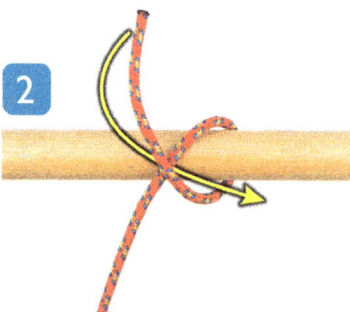

1) Wrap the running end around and behind the pole.

2) Wrap the running end around the front of the pole. Then, thread the running end between the loop and the pole.

3) Pull the running end loop away from the pole slightly.

4) Begin twisting the running end around itself to create a spiral.

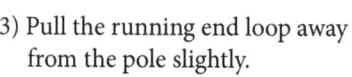

5) Tighten the knot by pulling on the standing part. The running end loop will compress and hold fast on a rough log or surface.

6) Tighten the hitch against the pole or log.

7) Add a Half Hitch to the standing part to stabilize the rope and make it easier to control the direction of the log being pulled.

Where & When to Use

The Timber Hitch is useful for pulling rough-surface logs and other cylindrical items. This knot doesn't bind at all and is easy to remove. Use it on any round or cylindrical objects to be dragged.

This hitch does not hold well on smooth surfaces. If you need to lift or drag a pipe, use the Pipe Hitch. Do not use the Timber Hitch for overhead lifting.

The Most Crucial Knots to Know

Trucker's Hitch

- Easy to untie
- Adjusts quickly
- Holds significant loads

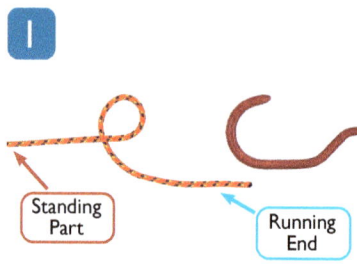

1) Create a loop with the running end over the standing part.

2) Create a bight in the running end and pass it through the loop to create a Slip Knot.

3) Wrap the running end around the attachment point.

4) Pass the running end through the Slip Knot loop.

5) Tension the standing part by pulling on the running end.

6) Tie a Half Hitch for non-critical loads to secure the hitch.

7) Tie Two Half-Hitches or half of a Fisherman's Bend for critical loads to secure the hitch.

Where & When to Use

The Trucker's Hitch, also known as the Power Cinch Knot, is the knot to use when you want to secure a load. Tie a canoe to a roof or float plane with this knot. The loop creates a pulley, generating a theoretical force of 3:1. Rope friction reduces this number in half but it still generates more force than just pulling a rope by itself. Tied properly, the knot will hold its place under vibration and load cycling.

Instead of a Slip Knot, other options for the fixed loop include using a Directional Figure 8, the Alpine Butterfly, the Bowline on a Bight, or the Figure 8 on a Bight. The version here with the Slip Knot is shown for its simplicity and ease of tying and untying.

The Most Crucial Knots to Know

Tumble Hitch

- Easy to tie
- Quick release hitch
- Works well on slippery surfaces

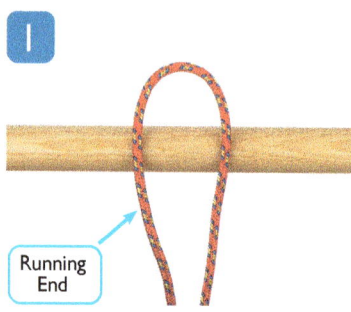

1) Place a loop over the object.

2) Create a bight in the running end.

3) Pass the bight under the object.

4) Thread the bight between the standing part loop and the object.

Aaron Linsdau

5) Create another bight in the running end and place it over the standing part. Pass the bight under the object. Thread the second bight through the first running end bight.

6) Pull on the standing part to tighten the knot. Pull on the running end to release the knot.

KNOTS

Where & When to Use

The Tumble Hitch is the close cousin of the Highwayman's Knot. The Tumble Hitch is arguably more secure on slippery surfaces or poles with modern slippery synthetic lines. Try both hitchs.

Of the two hitches, the Highwayman's Hitch is less complex and easier to inspect, as the bulk of the hitch is in front of the object. Leave a sufficient final loop to prevent the knot from slipping. Do not use this hitch for critical or overhead loads.

The Most Crucial Knots to Know

Two Half-Hitches

- Scouting knot
- Easy to release and untie
- Moderate holding power
- Create an adjustable loop

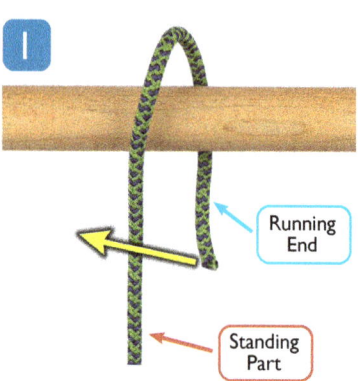 

1) Wrap the running end around the object. Lay the running end on top of the standing part to create a loop.

2) Thread the running end through the loop.

3) Lay the running end on the standing part outside of the loop.

4) Wrap the running end around the standing part and thread it through the second loop.

5) Dress the knot by snugging the pair of loops and pulling the running end until the loops are tight around the standing part.

6) Optional: Create a bight in the running end and thread it through the second loop in Step 5 to create a quick-release version.

Where & When to Use

The Two Half-Hitches is one of the easiest sliding loop knots to tie. It is highly versatile. It has moderate holding power while still being easy to adjust. However, it does not bind up and is easy to untie, due to the nature of the loop structure of the running end. To make the hitch more secure, wrap the running end around the object twice.

This knot is a Clove Hitch tied onto the standing part. This hitch is one of the fundamental Scouting knots. It is highly versatile, easy to tie, and easy to inspect. Due to the number of uses for this hitch, it is one everyone should know. Its utility at home, at camp, in survival, and rescue situations cannot be overstated.

 THE MOST CRUCIAL KNOTS TO KNOW

Water Knot

- Tie two straps together
- Connect two pieces of webbing
- Reliable for climbing and camping

 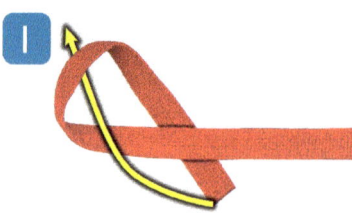

1) Start with the first strap and lay the running end behind the standing part. Then pass the running end through the loop to create an Overhand Knot.

2) The Overhand Knot is the basis for the Water Knot.

3) Lay the second strap parallel to the running end of the first strap.

4) Thread the running end of the second strap through the main loop of the first strap.

5) Continue tracing the running end of the first strap.

6) Make sure the straps lay flat against each other during the tracing process.

7) Thread the running end of the second strap through the main loop of the first strap and finish parallel to the first strap.

Where & When to Use

The Water Knot is the best and easiest knot to connect two straps or pieces of webbing together. Once the knot is heavily loaded, it will tighten on itself, making untying difficult.

With sufficient tails, this is an excellent knot to use for climbing. Leave long tails when used for fall protection during climbing.

As the knot is tightened, it will deform into a ball. This is normal and expected as the strap and webbing fabric deforms.

Always inspect this knot prior to use in any critical situations such as climbing or lifting overhead loads. Some webbing and many inexpensive strap materials can loosen over time. Always inspect straps, webbing, and knots prior to use.

 THE MOST CRUCIAL KNOTS TO KNOW

Diagonal Lashing

- Connect two separated poles
- Allows for non-perpendicular poles
- Great choice for diagonal cross members

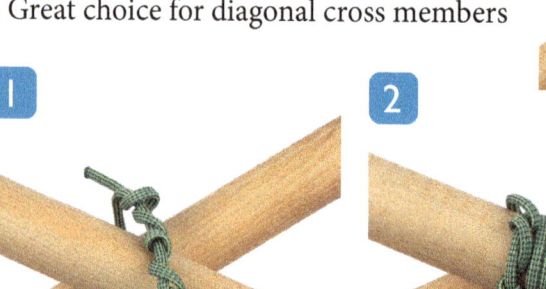

1

2

1) Start with a Timber Hitch around both poles and tighten the hitch to snug both poles together.

2) Make 3 tight wraps around the two poles, parallel to the Timber Hitch. Keep the wraps neat and snug.

3

4

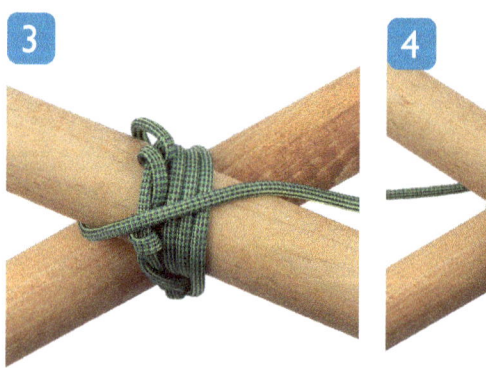

3) Change the wrapping direction and make 3 tight wraps that cross the first set of wraps.

4) Keep the wraps neat and snug.

5) Make 2-3 fraps (wraps between poles).

6) Finish the lashing off with a Clove Hitch backed up with a Two Half-Hitches or a Constrictor Knot.

Where & When to Use

The Diagonal Lashing is an excellent choice to connect poles that do not cross at 90°. This lashing has the strength to pull together two poles that are not touching but are close to each other. Tighten the frapping turns as much as possible to give the lashing strength.

The Timber Hitch start is important because it can compress two poles together. A Clove Hitch does not have that ability and will untie. For more permanence, use the Constrictor Knot to finish the lashing rather than the traditional Clove Hitch.

THE MOST CRUCIAL KNOTS TO KNOW

Round Lashing

- Create a rigid structure
- Extend the reach of poles
- Build an extended flag pole

1) Start with a Clove Hitch around both poles. Ensure that both poles are parallel and directly next to each other.

2) Make 10 wrapping turns around both poles. Lay the wraps neatly and make them as tight as possible, as they carry all the load.

3) Finish off the Round Lashing with a Clove Hitch.

4) Create a second Round Lashing as far away from the first lashing as possible to give the connection greater strength and stability.

Where & When to Use

The Round Lashing is one of the best choices for connecting two parallel poles. It can be used to make an extended flagpole of surprising height from a few poles.

The farther the second Round Lashing is placed from the first, the stronger the joint will be. Regularly inspect this lashing, as with all others, to ensure it has not loosened.

Slippery cord like 550 Paracord used on smooth poles will not hold the traditional starting and ending Clove Hitches well. Use a Constrictor Knot in place of both Clove Hitches for greater security and longevity.

Use this lashing to create an extended flag pole, signal pole, or to raise an antenna above the ground. This will help create improved signal reception and transmission.

THE MOST CRUCIAL KNOTS TO KNOW

Shear Lashing

- Weight bearing lashing
- Create a frame for lifting
- Create a cross-beam member

1) Start with a Clove Hitch around one of the poles.

2) Begin making wrapping turns around both poles.

3) Make 8-10 turns around both poles. Allow for a small amount of space between the poles.

Aaron Linsdau

4) Make two frapping turns, pulling them as tightly as possible. This will tighten the wrapping turns, gripping the poles. The poles may need to be spread apart to apply the frapping turns.

5) Finish off the Shear Lashing with a Clove Hitch.

Where & When to Use

The Sheer Lashing is an excellent choice for establishing the top of a triangle structure. Once the poles are separated, the lashing will tighten, creating substantial grip with the lashing rope and smooth poles. The Sheer Lashing can also support weight. Use this lashing to create an X-frame that can be used as a impromptu crane to lift items over an edge. A series of X-frames can be strung together to create a bridge over a swampy area.

This lashing can also be used to attach 3 poles together in the same manner. Place the third pole parallel to the second and add a set of frapping turns between the second and third poles.

 THE MOST CRUCIAL KNOTS TO KNOW

Square Lashing

- Create a structural member
- Connect two perpendicular poles
- Place a horizontal pole between two trees

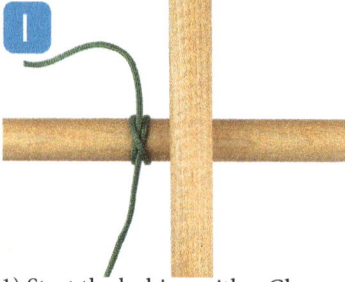

1) Start the lashing with a Clove Hitch on one of the poles.

2) Twist the spare running end around the wrapping line.

3) Create a series of wraps around both poles, above and then below each. Lay the successive wraps outside of each other, keeping them as tight as possible.

4) On the last wrapping turn, wrap the line around the finishing pole in preparation to create the frapping turns.

5) Create 3-4 frapping turns. Pull them as tight as possible to compress the wrapping turns against the poles.

6) Finish the lashing off with a Clove Hitch and a backup Two-Half Hitches as necessary.

Where & When to Use

The Square Lashing is the best choice when two poles touch each other and cross each other at close to 90°. The angle can be as little as 45°, though at that angle, the Diagonal Lashing becomes a better choice for connecting the poles.

Using the Square Lashing wrapping method, a floor of parallel poles can be built. Weave the line around the poles using the Square Lashing method to create a stable and strong floor.

The Clove Hitch for the beginning and end of the lashing may come untied on smooth poles with slippery line like 550 Paracord. As an alternative, start and end this lashing with a Constrictor Knot plus Two Half-Hitches for added safety.

 THE MOST CRUCIAL KNOTS TO KNOW

Tripod Lashing

- Create a tripod
- Hold a cooking pot
- Use as a leg for tables

1) Start the lashing with a Clove Hitch on one of the outside poles.

2) Weave the racking turns in and out of the three legs. Racking turns are woven rather than wrapping turns which are flat.

3) Create a series of 6-8 weaving racking turns around the legs. Too many turns makes it difficult to spread the legs.

4) Create 2 frapping turns around the first joint. Moderately tighten these frapping turns.

5) Create the second set of 2 frapping turns around the second joint. Again, moderately tighten the frapping turns.

Aaron Linsdau

6) Finish the lashing off with a Clove Hitch on the leg opposite the one with the starting Clove Hitch.

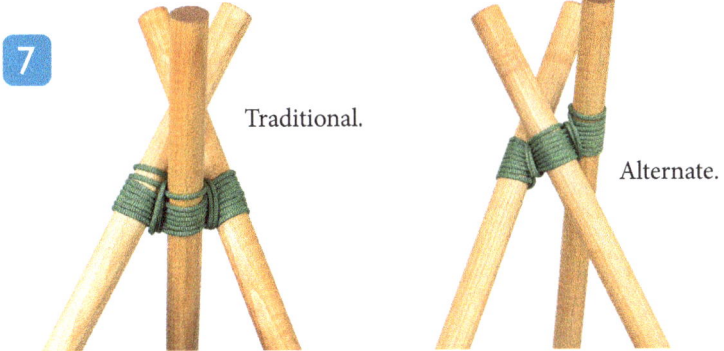

Traditional.

Alternate.

7) Spread the legs out. Stabilize the tripod with poles at the bottom lashed to the tripod feet with Diagonal Lashings. Multiple tripods can be combined to create tables with horizontal spars.

Where & When to Use

The Tripod Lashing is the cousin of the Shear Lashing. Tripod Lashing racking turns are woven rather than simply wrapped around the poles like the Shear Lashing. The woven turns make it possible to spread the three legs.

Some experimentation is required to establish the proper tension of the racking and frapping turns. If the turns and fraps are too tight, the rope can break from the tension force. If the turns are too loose, the poles will slide through the lashing and collapse the tripod. Test the strength of the tripod before committing a load, such as a cooking pot and dinner, to the structure.

 THE MOST CRUCIAL KNOTS TO KNOW

Back Splice

- Prevent unraveling
- Pass twisted rope through objects
- Finish off the end of a twisted rope

1) Unravel the rope far enough that the free strands fold back on the standing part at least 5 turns on the twists.

2) Create a Crown Knot by crossing two strands and wrapping the third strand over the adjacent strand and then under the farthest away strand.

ROPE CARE

3) Weave (tuck) each loose strand under the adjacent twist in the standing part of the rope. Tuck in the opposite direction of the twist in the standing part of the rope.

Aaron Linsdau

4) Continue reverse weaving the loose strands through the twists.

5) At the last weave, tuck the strands into the twisted strands on the standing part. Optionally, use a whipping to secure the loose strands.

Where & When to Use

The Back Splice is one of several options to secure the end of a twisted rope. This option is attractive and gives the rope a professionally manufactured look. Be aware that the extra thickness created by the reverse weaving will make passing the line through a pulley or block and tackle more difficult due to the increased thickness.

To create a Short Splice to permanently connect two rope ends together, use the same weaving method as the Back Splice. Undo the weave of both ropes a sufficient distance, then mate the trio of strands of one rope to another. Proceed to use the Back Splice weaving technique to connect the two ropes together. Add a minimum of 10 weaves if not more to ensure the rope will not pull apart.

Add a whipping to the tucked ends for additional security.

 THE MOST CRUCIAL KNOTS TO KNOW

Eye Splice

- Load securing
- Create a permanent loop
- Excellent way to end a woven rope

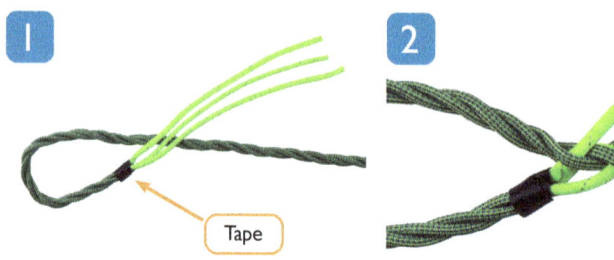

1) Unravel the rope far enough that the free strands fold back on the standing part at least 5 turns on the twists. Add tape to prevent the twists from unraveling farther.

2) Thread each loose strand under the adjacent twist in the standing part of the rope. It takes practice to make a clean start of a side entry of loose strands into the middle of a rope.

3) Start weaving (tucking) each loose strand under the adjacent twist in the standing part of the rope. Weave in the opposite direction of the twist in the standing part of the rope.

4) Continue reverse weaving (tucking) the loose strands through the twists in the standing part.

5) At the last weave (tuck), tuck the strands into the twisted strands on the standing part. Optionally, use a whipping to secure the loose strands.

Where & When to Use

The Eye Splice is an excellent choice to add a permanent loop to the end of a twisted rope. It is important to add a minimum of 5 reverse weaves (tucks) with the loose strands. For modern, slippery synthetic ropes, add 10 or more reverse weaves. This is especially important if semi-critical loads are to be carried.

For this illustration, 7 inches (18 cm) of twists were undone to complete the weaving. This resulted in 6 tucks. For important loads, the number of weaves (tucks) needs to be increased to 10 or more. There is no harm in adding a few more weaves to prevent the eye splice from pulling loose under heavy or sudden loads.

Add a whipping to the tucked ends for additional security.

 THE MOST CRUCIAL KNOTS TO KNOW

Whipping

- Prevents fraying
- Use to finish splices
- Protects the ends of a rope

ROPE CARE

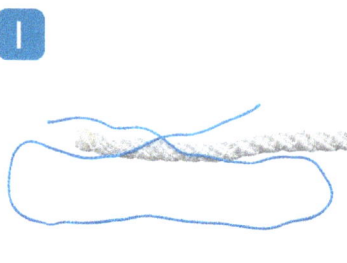

1) Start with the whipping string laid as a loop at the end of the rope to be finished.

2) Begin wrapping the top of the loop around the main rope.

3) Continue the wraps of the whipping until the length of the whipping is equal to or greater than the diameter of the rope.

4) Feed the free end of the whipping through the whipping loop.

5) Pull on the whipping line opposite of the loop to draw the end loop under the whipping wraps. Clip the ends of the whipping lines as close as possible to prevent snags.

6) Cut the rope to one rope diameter above the whipping. Melt the end of a synthetic rope, being careful not to damage the whipping.

Where & When to Use

This common whipping method is one of the easiest and fastest methods to finish the end of a rope. Adding a whipping is important for twisted rope, as this type of rope will naturally come undone without some type of finishing treatment. There are multiple styles of this whipping but this approach is the easiest to tie.

Other options to finish the end of a rope are the Eye Splice or the Back Splice. Be aware that each finish has its disadvantages. If one of the wraps of the whipping is damaged, it can unravel. A more secure but complex type of whipping is the Sailmaker's Whipping. This particular whipping will withstand damage and still hold together.

 THE MOST CRUCIAL KNOTS TO KNOW

Sled Towing Rig

- Reduce shock loading
- Tow a heavy sled in winter
- Reduce repetitive impact injuries

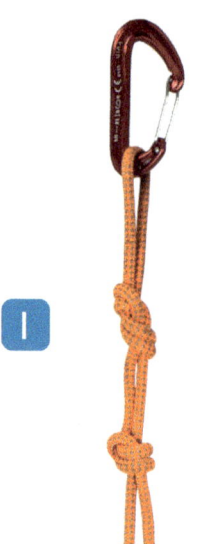

1) Tie a Figure 8 on a Bight on the trace line (line to tow with). Leave plenty of slack in the running end for adjustments. Tie the slack off with half of a Double Fisherman's Bend.

2) Tie a Figure 8 on the heavy bungee line. Use the Figure 8 Bend to tie together the trace line and the bungee. This knot will link them together and prevent disconnects.

3) Wrap the trace line around the bungee line in a double helix shape. Create another series of knots from Step 2 and then Step 1 to generate the other end of the Sled Towing Rig.

Where & When to Use

The Sled Towing Rig assembly allows a skier to haul hundreds of pounds (kilograms) of weight without injury. This method reduces the shock loading associated with pulling heavy sleds with an accessory cord.

This method requires a heavy-duty bungee line. An 11mm bungee and a 6mm accessory cord are shown in this illustration. Make this assembly at least 6 feet (183 cm) long to reduce the energy wasted lifting rather than pulling the load.

To improve efficiency, use a longer trace. Once the trace line is longer than 16 feet (4.9 m), the rope will bounce with every step which wastes energy.

This assembly works well in polar travel. When using only an accessory cord, every step will yank on a skier's back. By creating this double helix spiral, the impact is substantially reduced. The advantage of this design is the stretch is short compared to the bungee loop method or only using a bungee. This assembly keeps the skier tied to the sled in the event of a crevasse fall.

THE MOST CRUCIAL KNOTS TO KNOW

Swiss Seat

- Create harnesses for a team
- Make a harness out of thick rope
- Create an emergency climbing harness

1) Wrap a heavy line around your waist.

2) Tie the first part of the Square Knot.

3) Tie another wrap to create the first part of the Surgeon's Knot.

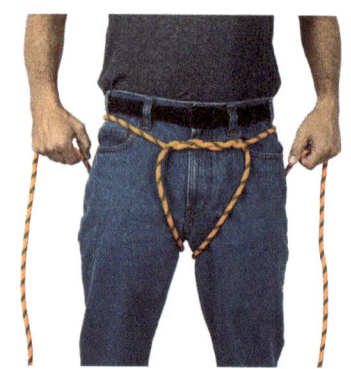
4) Wrap the two lines through your legs and hold them to the side.

5) Tighten the leg loops by pulling on both ends.

6) Thread the leg loops through and over the waist loop.

7) Tie an Overhand Knot with the leg loops on the waist loop.

8) Tighten the leg loops, pulling the Overhand Knots snug.

 THE MOST CRUCIAL KNOTS TO KNOW

9) Pull the right strand to the left side and tie the first part of a Square Knot with both strands.

10) Complete the Square Knot with both strands.

11) Tie off one strand with a Two Half-Hitches in front of the Square Knot from Step 10.

12) Tie off the second strand with a Two Half-Hitches behind the Square Knot and Overhand Knot.

13) Tie into the harness with a Figure Eight Follow Through or a locking carabiner and a Figure Eight on a Bight. Finish off the running end with an Overhand Knot or half of a Double Fisherman's Bend.

Where & When to Use

The Swiss Seat is the classic impromptu harness made out of heavy rope. Use the thickest rope possible, 9mm or thicker. Pay close attention to the finishing knots to ensure they remain tied.

As an added security, use half of the Double Fisherman's Bend in Step 11 and Step 12 to tie off the leg loops. The classic Swiss Seat design is shown in this illustration but the Double Fisherman's Bend finish is more secure.

The Most Crucial Knots to Know

Texas Prusik

- Emergency escape
- Climb out of a crevasse
- Ascend a rope without aid devices

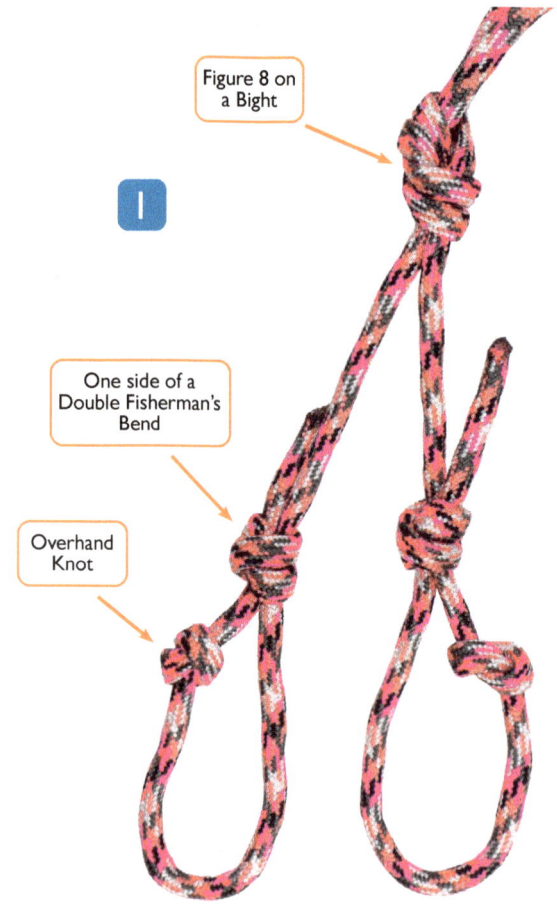

1) Tie a Figure Eight on a Bight on the lower foot ascent cords. Tie an Overhand Knot on each line. Then, take the running end and tie one side of a Double Fisherman's Bend. This creates a foot loop. The Overhand Knot prevents the Double Fisherman's Bend from over-tightening on your footwear.

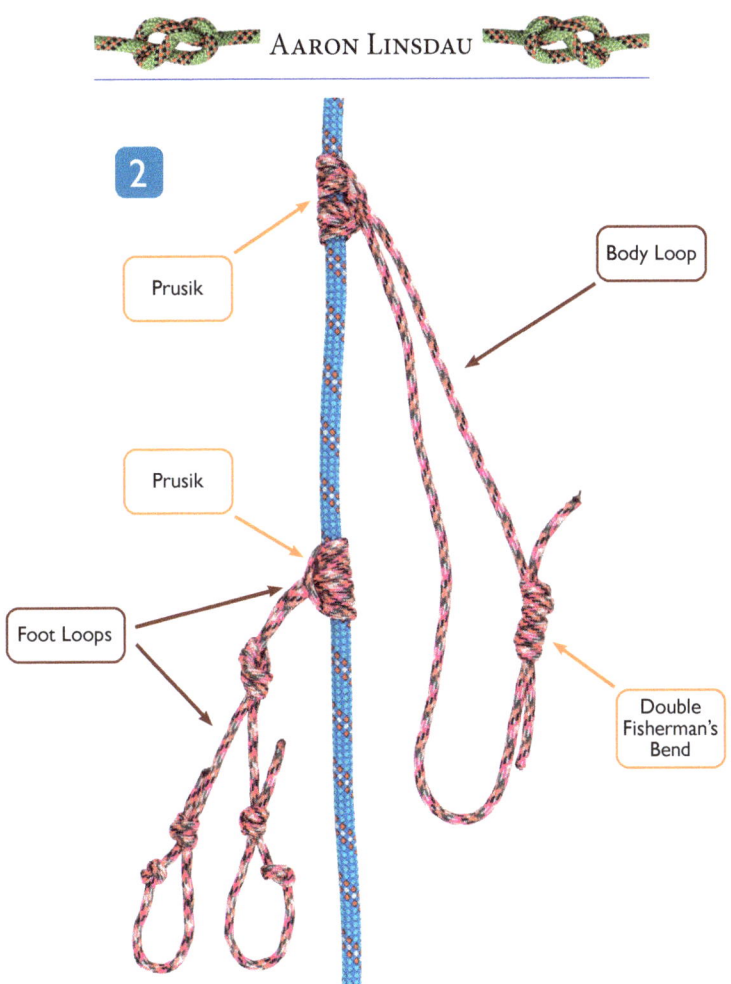

2) Tie the foot loops to the static line with a Prusik. Tie another loop with a Double Fisherman's Bend and then attach that loop with a Prusik to the static line above the foot loops.

Where & When to Use

The Texas Prusik is a combination of several knots and hitches to create a rope ascending system when mechanical aid devices are unavailable. This method requires a climbing harness, ideally a commercial harness, or the Swiss Seat in an emergency.

The method of ascent is to stand on the two foot loops, then raise the body loop up a short distance. Then, place the body weight on the body loop and bring your knees up to your chest. Slide the foot loop Prusik up, then stand on the loops. Repeat the process.

The Most Crucial Knots to Know

Rope Care & Types

Rope Care

Modern ropes are highly durable and fairly UV (ultraviolet) light-resistant. If properly cared for, lightly-used ropes will provide many years of service. Paying a valuable rope a few moments of attention will make all the difference in how long a rope lasts.

Follow the manufacturer's suggestion for life expectancy. Since ropes are used for so many critical purposes, suggested lifetimes are often highly conservative. Avoid stepping on a rope, as this drives sharp crystals into the invisible core of the rope, cutting critical fibers. The damage is insidious and cumulative.

Once a rope is damaged or takes a heavy shock load (fall factor 2), replace it immediately. Although ropes can be expensive, your life and property are not worth the cost of a rope. Often the damage to a rope's internal fibers cannot be seen. When in doubt, throw it out.

Treating a climbing rope well is especially important, as it protects climbers from serious or fatal falls. Do not use climbing ropes for car towing or anything other than climbing. Keep these ropes knot-free, dry, out of sunlight, and in a loose storage bag.

Should a climbing rope become excessively dirty, hand wash it with gentle soap and thoroughly rinse it out. Do not use any type of heat source to dry the rope and keep it out of sunlight. Gently loop a climbing rope back and forth inside a storage room off the floor and only use a fan to facilitate drying. Refer to the manufacturer's datasheet on when to retire a climbing rope.

Rope Types

Cotton: This is an excellent choice for crafting. Cotton rope is inexpensive and is pleasant to handle. It does not hold up well over time to abuse and outdoor environments.

Kevlar: Kevlar ropes are extremely strong and handle high heat, up to 500°F (260°C). Kevlar rope has low stretch. However, Kevlar has a poor UV resistance, so it is often sheathed in polyester rope.

Manila (and other natural fiber ropes): This rope is unaffected by heat and is highly resistant to UV light. However, this rope will rot if left wet over time.

Nylon: It is highly abrasion resistant, durable, handles well, rot-resistant, and handles shock load. It returns to its original length after stretching. Nylon rope is the easiest to tie knots with. However, it degrades in UV and does not handle heat, as it weakens at 350ºF (177ºC). Overheated belay devices can cause invisible damage to nylon climbing ropes. Nylon rope also sags when wet. Blended nylon and polyester ropes combine the positive traits of both materials.

Polyester: This rope is acid-resistant, durable, rot-resistant, low-stretch, and retains its strength when wet. It is less flexible than nylon rope but is an excellent choice for marine applications and clotheslines. Polyester-based and nylon blended ropes are arguably the best all-around choice for general use.

Polypropylene: It floats, is resistant to chemicals, and handles wet climates well. It melts at low temperatures and has low UV and abrasion resistance. This is an excellent choice for applications requiring a floating rope or harsh chemical environments.

Rope Construction

Braided: Easy to handle and does not unravel easily.
Kernmantle: Best for climbing and general applications.
Stranded (Twisted): Best for creating splices. The twists add friction over surfaces for improved grip, especially with hitches.

THE MOST CRUCIAL KNOTS TO KNOW

Knot Tying Scenarios

Clothesline setup
Start with a Bowline on one end, then use the Trucker's Hitch on the other end to create a tensioned clothesline.

Create a loop in the middle of a rope
Use the Alpine Butterfly Knot to create a single, non-sliding loop in the middle of a rope. Use the Bowline on a Bight to create a pair of symmetric non-sliding loops in the middle of a rope.

Connect two twisted ropes together
Use the Short Splice described in the Back Splice When & Where to Use section.

Connect two synthetic sheathed ropes together
For light-duty use with simple removal, the Sheet Bend is easy and quick to tie. For semi-permanent critical applications, use the Double Fisherman's Bend. For critical applications where minimal knot bulk is needed, the Overhand Bight with plenty of tail is a good choice for an emergency rappel (abseil).

Drag a log
To drag a log, use the Timber Hitch with an additional Half Hitch to guide the log. Avoid having anyone stand near the sliding log, as they can tumble unexpectedly.

Improvised belt
Use the Shoelace Bow or the Square Knot with rope to hold up a pair of pants when a belt is unavailable.

Improvised hose or pipe clamp
Use the Constrictor Knot and thin, synthetic line as an emergency hose or pipe clamp. This knot works incredibly well at holding onto rounded surfaces. It tensions so well it often has to be cut to be removed.

Lift a pipe or pole

To lift a slippery pipe or pole, use the Pipe Hitch along with a Half Hitch to guide the load. Prevent anyone from being under the load while it is being lifted to avoid injury.

Pitch a camping tarp

For the classic pup tent tarp setup, use two poles to suspend the centerline of the tarp. Tie a Figure 8 on a Bight to the middle of a guyline and attach the loops to the top of the poles. Use the Taut-Line hitch on each end of the guyline and attach them to stakes.

For the tarp corners, attach guylines to the tarp with Two Half-Hitches. Tie Taut-Line Hitches to the stake end of the guylines.

Pitch a tent

Connect the guyline to the tent with Two Half-Hitches. On the stake end of the guyline, use the Taut-Line Hitch to make the line tension adjustable.

Pull a vehicle out of a ditch

Using a heavy rope, tie a Figure 8 Follow Through Loop to a tree and a Bowline Knot (with half of a Double Fisherman's Bend as backup) to a solid towing point on the vehicle. Stand in the middle of the rope and pull perpendicular (90º) to the rope. The force vector generated will often be enough to pull the car out. Use a Trucker's Hitch with a metal ring instead of a Slip Knot as an alternative.

Repair a drape pull cord

Use a Sheet Bend or a Square Knot, whichever holds on the cord.

Repair a wooden garden stake

Using thin twine, start with a Constrictor Knot at one end of the splintered stake. Wrap the line around the stake, then finish it off with another Constrictor Knot.

Rock climbing

Always tie into a commercial climbing harness with the Figure 8 Follow Through Loop with a backup knot. There is no other generally accepted safe choice for climbing.

The Most Crucial Knots to Know

Survival tarp setup

To set up a lean-to survival shelter, tie a heavy rope between two trees using a Bowline or Figure 8 on a Bight on one end and a Trucker's Hitch on the other. Create several rope loops with 550 Paracord.

Tie each Paracord loop to the heavy rope with a Prusik Knot and tension the tarp. Then, pass the loop through the grommet of the tarp and use a stick as a toggle. For a more secure method instead of the toggle, use the Highwayman's Hitch to connect to the tarp grommets.

Tie a box closed

Using thin twine, wrap around a box and then tie both ends together with a Square Knot.

Tie a bag closed

Use thin twine and use the Miller's Knot to tie the bag closed. For a more permanent closure, use the Constrictor Knot. The twine may need to be cut to release the bag.

Tie a kayak or canoe to a car roof or a floatplane

Tie a Bowline with a backup half of a Fisherman's Bend to one attachment point on the car. Weave the rope back and forth across the canoe or kayak, making sure to pass the rope around the canoe thwarts and seats or the equivalent permanent points on the kayak.

Use the Trucker's Hitch to tension the rope on the second attachment point on the car. Finish it off with an extra Two Half-Hitches or half of a Double Fisherman's Bend for long distance travel. Test the stability before driving or flying.

Tie a load in a pickup truck

Tie a Two Half-Hitch or a Bowline with backup to the first attachment point in the pickup truck bed. Weave the rope across the load appropriately. Use the Trucker's Hitch to create tension on the rope and tie it off with an extra Two Half-Hitches or half of a Double Fisherman's Bend for critical loads.

Tie a loop in the middle of a rope

Use the Alpine Butterfly for a single loop or the Bowline on a Bight to create a double loop.

Survival Tips

Fire starting tinder
The fine fibers that make up synthetic rope are an excellent fire starting tinder. Take a short section of rope and tear it apart to the individual threads. Create a loose bundle similar in density to a cotton ball. Prepare the rest of the fire with this tinder, kindling, and fuel at the ready. Apply a spark or flame to the makeshift tinder.

Fishing (Gill) Net
Pull the core lines from a length of a 550 Paracord, triple the width of the desired net. Tie the casing line (from which the core lines have been removed) between two trees with a Mooring Hitch on either end. Use a Girth Hitch or Prusik Knot to tie the midpoint of each core line to the outside casing. Space the core lines 1-2 inches (3-6 cm) along the outside casing. Tie adjacent core lines with a Flat Overhand Bend or a Sheet Bend to create a diamond pattern gill net. Finish the outside edges of the net with additional Paracord casings.

River crossing
Find the shallowest, slowest crossing point possible. Release all of the backpack buckles in case of a stumble. Tie a rope to the first person crossing with a Bowline with a backup knot. Have the team hold the first person's line in case the person loses their footing.

Splint a broken limb
Use boards, heavy sticks, trekking poles, or tent poles and place them on either side of the limb. Wrap straps or rope around the limb and finish the ends off with a Square Knot.

Trapping & Snaring
In a long-term survival situation, food will become an issue. Take the core strands of quality 550 Paracord and use them to trap or snare small game. Use the Honda Knot for the snare. Always respect local hunting and trapping regulations.

Enjoy Other Books by Aaron Linsdau

Black Ice

Some missions don't have a way back. When a hypersonic drone crashes in northern Finland, Grant Colson races against the elements and unseen dangers before the mission, and his team, are erased by the Arctic. *Free book.*
www.aaronrlinsdau.com/sera/black-ice/

The Magellan Deception

A secret was lost on Magellan's last voyage. Forged from a metal once sought by empires, it holds the power to shift the world order. As the trail resurfaces, Grant Colson and Luis Fontaine race to stop a discovery from turning history into a weapon.

www.aaronrlinsdau.com/grant-colson-series/the-magellan-deception/

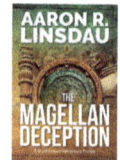

Adventure Expedition One
by Aaron Linsdau M.S. & Terry Williams, M.D.

Create, finance, enjoy, and return safely from your first expedition. Learn the techniques explorers use to achieve their goals and have a good time doing it. Acquire the skills, find the equipment, and learn the planning necessary to pull off an expedition.
www.sastrugipress.com/books/adventure-expedition-one/

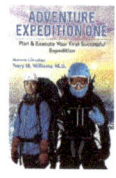

Antarctic Tears

Experience the honest story of solo polar exploration. This inspirational true book will make readers both cheer and cry. Coughing up blood and fighting skin-freezing temperatures were only a few of the perils Aaron Linsdau faced. Travel with him on a world-record expedition to the South Pole.
www.sastrugipress.com/books/antarctic-tears/

Jackson Hole Hiking Guide

Jackson Hole contains some of the most dramatic and iconic landscapes in the United States. The book shares everything you need to know to hike Jackson's classic trails with canyons, high mountains, and hidden alpine lakes. This book is an excellent companion guide to *50 Jackson Hole Photography Hotspots.*
www.sastrugipress.com/books/jackson-hole-hiking-guide/

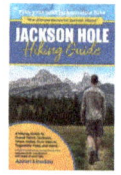

Subscribe to Aaron's YouTube channel: www.youtube.com/@alinsdau

If you enjoyed this book, please consider leaving a review and a few words on what you liked about it at your favorite online retailer.

Lost at Windy Corner

Windy Corner on Denali has claimed fingers, toes, and even lives. What would make someone brave lethal weather, crevasses, and avalanches to attempt to summit North America's highest mountain? Aaron Linsdau shares the experience of climbing Denali alone and how you can apply the lessons to your life.

www.sastrugipress.com/books/lost-windy-corner/

The Motivated Amateur's Guide to Winter Camping

Winter camping is one of the most satisfying ways to experience the wilderness. It is also the most challenging style of overnighting in the outdoors. Learn 100+ tips from a professional polar explorer on how to winter camp safely and be comfortable in the cold.

www.sastrugipress.com/books/the-motivated-amateurs-guide-to-winter-camping/

Two Friends and a Polar Bear
by Terry Williams, M.D. & Aaron Linsdau

Winter camping is one of the most satisfying ways to experience the wilderness. It is also the most challenging style of overnighting in the outdoors. Learn 100+ tips from a professional polar explorer on how to winter camp safely and be comfortable in the cold.

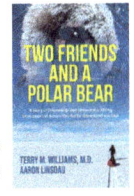

www.sastrugipress.com/books/two-friends-and-a-polar-bear/

About the Author

Aaron Linsdau is the second American to ski alone from the coast of Antarctica to the South Pole (730 miles / 1174 km), setting a world record for surviving the longest expedition ever for that trip. He lead a 310-mile (499 km) ski expedition across the Greenland icecap along the Arctic Circle. Aaron has climbed Denali solo, crossed the Greenland tundra alone, skied across Yellowstone National Park solo, trekked through the Sahara desert, and has climbed on Denali, the Matterhorn, Mt. Kilimanjaro, and Mt. Elbrus in Russia.

Aaron Linsdau at the South Pole.

Use your smart device to scan the QR codes for website links.

Visit www.aaronrlinsdau.com to learn more about the author. Receive updates when he releases new books and shows.

Visit Sastrugi Press on the web at www.sastrugipress.com to purchase the above titles in bulk. They are available in print, e-book, or audiobook form.

Thank you for choosing Sastrugi Press.

www.ingramcontent.com/pod-product-compliance
Lightning Source LLC
La Vergne TN
LVHW050732250326
834741LV00025B/183/J